T0104052

RED SHADOWS OF THE BLOOD MOON

JOHN WESLEY CONTWAY

Order this book online at www.trafford.com
or email orders@trafford.com

Most Trafford titles are also available at major online book retailers.

Print information available on the last page.

ISBN: 978-1-4907-6849-6 (sc)
ISBN: 978-1-4907-6851-9 (hc)
ISBN: 978-1-4907-6850-2 (e)

Library of Congress Control Number: 2015921375

Trafford rev. 01/11/2016

Trafford PUBLISHING® www.trafford.com
North America & international
toll-free: 1 888 232 4444 (USA & Canada)
fax: 812 355 4082

Acknowledgments

I would like to thank my informal support team for all they have done to help me. I would like to thank Carlyn Jensen Ramsey, who I love unconditionally for saving my life, and making me go to the hospital against my will. She completed the first edit while I was still writing and shortened the book into two full manuscripts. I wish to thank Margaret Galovin for her edits and pushing me onward when I had given up. I also want to extend a huge thanks and appreciation to my dear friend Barbara Graham for not letting me quit. Without her selfless dedication and full edit, the completion of this manuscript "Red Shadows of the Blood Moon" might not have been completed.

Foreword

Red Shadows of the Blood Moon is a wild ass psychedelic tale from a Native American psycho-social perspective. It is a story of a bi-cultural family's survival throughout the Native American genocide in Montana during the 19th Century. A first generation Irishman from Pottsville Pennsylvania, Bartholomew Ball, fought for the Union Army during the Civil War. Following the war, his post traumatic experience brought him West against his family's wishes. Amidst the Native American holocaust, he took Wakan Lokahe Win (First Holy Woman) as his wife. She was forced to change her name to a white name, Mary Jane Ball, forever losing her Lakota identity; generations of lost identities ensued. This is a story of historical trauma, a family's entropic breakdown, survival and resilience through four generations following the genocide.

This book is dedicated to our Spirit Creator, Big Medicine, 'Qua Quia'. It is in memoriam to our Lakota great great grandfather Itate' (Windy Mouth), Sitting Bull and Crazy Horse, with stories about the legacy of our great grandparents, Bartholomew Ball and Mary Jane 'Wakan Lokahe Win' Ball. It is the oral tradition memories of our grandmothers, grandfathers and our parents who brought us here, a tribute to the brothers and sisters we have chosen, and a journey of 'blood brothers' through the dichotomous two worlds of a distorted parallel universe.

Chapter 1

Before the World Began

It was a spring day of the vernal equinox when I arrived in this alien life from the ancient world. I felt my lungs fill with oxygen, listened to the ghost voices as the doctor spanked my ass with a sterile rubber gloved hand to jump start my fragile lungs. I started to scream. The red darkness filled my primitive thoughts and ambivalent mind. It hadn't yet been filled with the voices of doubt and fear. That came with time. I searched for my ancestral Lakota determination. I heard primeval voices of the Anasazi, Hohokam, and Moggolon. I heard the Elders' spoken words before my birth, before their birth, voices of our ancient people. My first cognition was watching the blue curtains blowing in the wind, and hearing the voices of their ancient carnal thoughts. I saw an indistinguishable face, as soft as the breeze. It sang a song of many dreams. The songs drifted across the years, decades and generations. The melodies of pride were met with the harmony of loss, grief, shame and the ghost dance challenges still to come. Perhaps it was a 60's impairment, or a warp in the space-time continuum.

I had a dream sent from my ancestors, my name was Tatanka Mato Itate', given to me by the great white father in that world...I am nobody in this one. I see you walk past me, I am invisible in the white world, and you do not care to see me in mine. You hold rather tightly to your misguided beliefs about our people. We are *red shadows*; we are the American shame of your white privilege... the denial of your genocidal humanity.

Tatanka Íyotake's spirit spoke to me at a Catholic mission when I was four years old; it was 1958 in the mountains of western Montana in the Mission Valley. Uncle Ervin and my dad took me to meet the white buffalo named Big Medicine. He was shaking his shaggy head, flailing, snorting a frosty chill defiantly into the crisp morning air. The depth of his power was overwhelming as I stared into his haunted steely blue eyes. His massive being embodied the souls of our ancient ancestors whose spirits still walk the earth. Qua Quia is symbolic of future events, even wearing their hides transcended the Medicine Man to the spirit world. I wanted to cry but I stood there, still and frozen in time.

I heard the oral history from birth as I listened to my parents, aunties and uncles. They often visited around my mother's round wooden oak table laughing and joking into the early dawn. The women drank black Lipton Tea or Folgers Coffee and worried. The men drank Lucky Lager, Seagram's 7 and boasted. They told family stories remembered from childhood and their parents' childhood before them, long before they were born. I first heard the stories of my great-great grandfather Itate' when I was an infant. The white men called him 'Windy Mouth'. To his people, Itate' was the voice of the four holy winds. He was a tall man who spoke many languages and shared many teepees. The winds waited for his direction in their travels; the people listened to his voice for guidance to the winter hunt. He was a warrior with the love and admiration of the clan and his woman, Winpagi -Wan Mni

Awacin. She was the envy of every young woman in the tribe. Above all, Itate' was a protector of the helpless, the elders and children. He fought fiercely in battle and spoke peace in his heart. Itate' carried wisdom spoken only to the chosen Lakota warriors.

Itate' was a mentor to the young light-eyed Indian warrior, Tshunke Witko. Crazy Horse is known to the white man as a huge stone rock monument in the Dakota Territories. A crazy white man's vision told Ziolkowski to build it. They take donations to capture Tshunke Witko's soul in stone, but his soul will not surrender. Crazy Horse was born in 1843 during the blood moon, three years before my great grandmother, First Holy Woman. As children they played hiding games on the sagebrush covered prairie in fear of capture by the white cavalry soldiers who were becoming more frequent in the Dakota Territories. Crazy Horse grew up with the instinct for war; he narrowly survived death on many occasions. His size, speed and cunning elevated him to a war leader of the Oglala band of the Lakota as he grew into adulthood. He was recognized by his light colored curly hair that flew behind him riding into the heat of battle.

My great uncle Tatanka Íyotake, was born in the Lakota Territories in 1831. He was like the big brother when Tshunke Witko and my great grandmother Wakan Lokahe Win were children. He carried himself with confidence and assurance. His charisma gained him the respect of both friends and enemies. He was known to General George Armstrong Custer as Sitting Bull, a visionary man of the feared ancient Ghost Dance spirits.

The Ghost Dance was an ancient ritual prophesied across the nations by a half-breed Piute named Wovoka. The prophecy called for the return of ancient ancestor spirits to wash away the white man from the land. We are here in this world born of ashes from a fire that burns flames of ice. These warriors and Qua Quia are the source of the Lakota spirit, my belief in the spirit world, my trust in the world beyond this one. It is a huge task to live in this world with meaning and intent.

It was the winter freeze of 1846 in the Dakota Territories during the holy moon east of the devil's lake when my great grandmother, First Holy Woman, Wakan Lokahe Win, was born to Itate' and Wan Mni Awacin, in their lodge. Wan Mni Awacin was the daughter of Thinking of an Eagle and 'Winpagi' Brown Hair Woman of the Sisseton.

Wakan Lokahe Win was to become a healer woman, yet she was known to my great grandfather, Bartholomew, only as Mary Jane Ball. That was where our test began. She was no longer allowed to be Lakota. She was re-named Mary after my white great-great grandmother. Her middle name came from great aunt Jane in order to make First Holy Woman 'more Irish.' After all, she couldn't be more Indian.

First Holy Woman was three years older than the warrior, Gall. He was born in 1849 near the Black Hills, during the summer camp while the tribe was hunting and fishing along Elk Creek. She knew him growing up in the Dakota Territories from the time he was a boy. Their paths crossed again in the Lakota winter camps when she was a young girl. Gall was a young Lakota, like a massive young grizzly. He was a great warrior destined to be war chief. Gall was mostly a 'mamma's boy', an efficiency expert due to his laziness. He thought like the bear and could be as deadly. His strike was fierce and fatal. Gall was destined to experience the extreme polarization of the buffalo spirit in his political separation from Sitting Bull after the end of the Indian wars.

Generations later, as a 4-year-old boy, I internalized the Big Medicine buffalo spirit as I stared into his eyes, the assimilation and accommodation of my genetic predisposition… 'Look down on no one; look up at no one'.

I chose my ancestors' fight against institutional oppression and the genocide of the Lakota cultures. There exists an insidious fear shared by white people for the primitive red man. I find it humiliating, at times being lost in the sea of foreign strangers that inhabit our land. They disregard our values and replace them with the stereotype of the pride-less drunken Indian. The time I spent learning to be poor was only preparation for understanding, through my struggle with addictions, through transgenerational implicit bias, through college and social work, always looking to understand why. It was my destiny…I had no choice in the matter. A planned life direction was impossible, a series of random accidents which were determined by ghosts of our great grandfathers. Sometimes the solutions were profound, sometimes miserable failures.

My mother and Aunt Nora sat drinking Lipton iced tea from mason jars in the hot sunbaked summer afternoon. Uncle Jim was on a drunk. My aunt and cousin Belle came to visit for the afternoon. Nora worried about Uncle Jim burning himself up in the old shack if he rolled a Bull Durham cigarette and passed out. The conversation was soon detoured by telling stories about First Holy Woman and the lifetime of instability that our family had overcome.

My great grandmother was said to have been a deer spirit… an elusive, gentle and strong woman. She was no easy match for Bartholomew. She could out-stubborn him with her Missouri mule headed disposition when she was determined. The story goes that she was bought, stolen or traded by a Civil War soldier when she was a young girl. I learned that the perpetrator was my great grandfather, Bartholomew. He was born in July of 1845 in a place called Pennsylvania.

Bartholomew Ball joined the white man army in 1863 during the great American Civil War. He enlisted as a soldier in the Pennsylvania 31st Regiment, U.S. Infantry. He did not come away unscathed, forever carrying the post-traumatic stress disorder implicit in the act of war. Mary Jane was often the brunt of his anger during the episodes. She carried her own trauma wounds that were implicit in the act of the extermination of her culture.

Ball was a first generation Irish 'Mick' who had come to this country in hopes of finding his American dream. He was a tall thin man with a hooked Irish nose. Those blue eyes lit up with a joke, and he grinned like an overgrown leprechaun when he was in a playful mood.

Unfortunately, Bartholomew found entertainment in drinking Irish whiskey and 'kicking the dog'. His family never knew which was coming first or from what direction.

After Bartholomew narrowly escaped the barrage of southern desperation at Bull Run, he found his way to Gettysburg. The sound of war ceased, but the echo shook him from his innocence. Unable to return to the blasé life of Pottsville, Bartholomew followed the government soldiers to the Montana Territories during the Indian Wars.

He spent most of his time dodging firefights between Indian war parties and the U.S. Calvary. The conflict escalated across the plains as hatred and greed consumed the white Americans in their desire for Lakota land. It was land that made them feel important and whole people in their own eyes. Around the world, white people had a need to own the land and own the many shades of black and yellow people who lived on it. They couldn't figure out how to own red people. Today, the ownership is in the Individual Indian Monies (IIM) trust accounts. Indian people have lost their dreams. It extends no further than Walmart and their immediate gratification. Indian people have been denied so long, they scramble like dogs for a bone before it is taken from them. They fight each other for leftover scraps from the Bureau of Indian Affairs.

After stealing Wakan Lokahe Win in the middle of the night, my great grandfather married First Holy Woman in the early 1860's at the Fort Peck Wolf Point outpost on their journey west to Fort Assiniboine. Itate' was hot on Ball's trail for dishonoring his daughter. There was a lance meant for his cowardly Irish white man heart. The government agent insisted that she have a white name when they got married. Bartholomew gave her his mother's and sister's first names; she was now Mary Jane Ball, leaving the Lakota world behind. Narrowly escaping Itate' again, they rode off into the night westward toward the Milk River valley.

Bartholomew and his property, First Holy Woman, set out on horseback from the Dakotas for the northern plains of the Montana Territories. They carried what they could; he hunted and she gathered the prairie harvest along the trail to Fort Assiniboine. The late 1880's were filled with terror and destruction for the Lakota and all native tribes. Villages were raided, burned and destroyed with the westward movement. The onslaught continued from the east coast to the west. It displaced tribes from their river valleys and mountain meadows as far as a gun and cannon could kill and conquer.

Death raged across the 'human beings' hunting territory. The terrorist insurgents slaughtered 83 million buffalo, the Indian life source…our Creator Spirit. The white man killed 63 million men, women and children while building this country at the turn of the 20th Century. They still take great industrial pride in their accomplishments. Left behind were the glory legends of men like Buffalo Bill Cody, tales of our great American history from a white supremacist memory of honor and valor. Meanwhile, white men fought white men so black men could be free. There were occasionally black men who passed through the territories. They were also spirit brothers of the buffalo and they made friends easily in most Indian communities. Some of them came with the U.S. Army, and some came looking for their white freedom, though not many came; freedom cost a lot in those days. As property values continued to rise, trust was always a risky thing for these 'buffalo men'.

They were hesitant of the Lakota at first because they did not trust the Cherokee, the civilized tribes, who made slaves of the black people if they were caught. White men made slaves of Cherokee women and made them their wives if they were caught. The white masters brought them to this country in wooden slave ships, kept them in irons and then expected them to be free. Laws don't make men free, only the Creator can set man free in his own good time. Freedom comes as winter settles in his heart and he is at peace with the seasons.

The Dakota tribes would not reach that point of contemplation in the late 1800's. They sent Little Crow, a Dakota chief from Minnesota, to Washington DC to convince the powers that be to enforce existing treaties. Unsuccessful, they lost the north half of the Minnesota River, and the settlers took their sacred Pipestone Quarry, a place that all tribes had considered as neutral for centuries to collect the pipestone for their ceremonies. Their same land was plotted for settlers, the railroad and logging which ended the Dakota's yearly migration of hunting, fishing, farming and gathering grains.

The tribes were losing their way of life and their ability to sustain themselves by trading. The government promised payment for what was lost, but "forgot" to pay. Little Crow's people, disheartened by broken promises and famine, took the matter into their own hands and decided to attack the settlements to scare the white man away from their tribal property. After one last attempt asking to buy food for their starving children on credit, the Southern Agency's government man turned them away saying, "So far as I am concerned, if they are hungry let them eat grass or their own dung." So began the short lived Dakota War of 1862.

It began in August, and by the end of September, 303 of Little Crow's men surrendered. All of these men were found guilty in trials that lasted five minutes each. The 28 Lakota men were executed by a decree of President Lincoln and hanged only to make the settlers happy. Their scalps were cut off and sold, then later the mass grave they were dumped in was dug up at night and their bodies given to area doctors to cut up.

Just a week before the signing of the Emancipation Proclamation on January 1, 1863, the Dakota lost all their land and were shipped south like cattle. Any indigenous person found in the area from then on was to be killed and a reward of $25 per scalp would be paid. Their prized bones were kept in museums and by the Mayo clinic until late in the 20th century.

It was a sad day across the territories when the great white father, Mr. Lincoln, lost his life to another white man. His enemies killed him without hesitation when he gave the buffalo brothers their freedom by the white man law. His enemies killed him in the dark of night, shielded from their deeds and black hearts. If only his enemies had not killed him, perhaps he would have finally understood and made all of the 'human beings' free men.

Instead, Indians were taken by train to the Auschwitz and Dachau internment in the Nebraska Territories.

During the Indian Wars, Bartholomew Ball worked off and on as a blacksmith at Fort Assiniboine in north-central Montana near the Bear Paw Mountains. His drinking became excessive; he brutalized Mary Jane and blamed her for his despair. They stayed until the decimation of the last buffalo herds, including the genocide of most of the Indians. She wanted to go home, but she had no home to go to. Her family was scattered in the wake of the holocaust. The destruction left entire civilized cultures annihilated at the hand of the Great White Father's U.S. Government. They are never to be trusted. To this day, we don't trust white people. You never know whether they may be bureaucrats who continue the surreptitious genocide as they smile to our faces. They are all the same you know, white, pale and stale. Bartholomew was stuck between two worlds too, being a 'squaw-man' he was forced to defend his own blood from the hatred and ridicule of both sides.

As the atrocities waxed and waned during the second half of the 19th Century, the Great White Fathers perpetrated their ongoing genocidal humanity which instilled the 'human beings' fear and hatred for the terrorist insurgents. Repeated incidents became familiar, the reported massacres of helpless innocent women, children and elders. The blood spread across the Montana and Dakota Territories. The bloodshed was soon to be forgotten, plowed under and turned to sod on a family farm without the blink of an eye. More than 700 U.S. Calvary soldiers killed 170 Cheyenne in November, 1864, mostly elders, women and children, at the Sandy Creek massacre in the Colorado Territories. This terrorist insurgency unified the Indian people's determination to fight the fiercest battles for the survival of their cultural and spiritual freedoms.

Chapter 2

Milk River Clay and the Coyote

First Holy Woman never bothered to learn English and Bartholomew never found a reason to speak Lakota. They learned to communicate in non-verbal 'high context' language from years of familiarity, the way all families know from a glance when a certain line has been crossed. Mary Jane let him know when she was not happy with his behavior with the same familiar stern look my mother gave me that stopped me in my tracks. Although Mary Jane, First Holy Woman, was as stern as a Lakota war pony, she held fast to her kindness of heart and maternal Lakota ways, showing her softness when caring for children, the wounded and the helpless. After the buffalo were gone the weary Indian families had nowhere to go but to the reservation without hope, starving and beaten. Bartholomew claimed his government land and asserted his white privilege near Lodge Pole. His homestead was known as Ball's Canyon.

That's where my mother grew up with her eight brothers and sisters. They lived there until the death of Bartholomew and Mary Jane. Our family became foreigners in this land once they died and Ball's Canyon was deeded back to the Fort Belknap reservation.

My Aunt Sis, mom's oldest sister, was the family historian and knower of all things from the white man world. She was the matriarch of the family, even though as an adult she didn't live in reservation poverty, or worse, white poverty. She gulped her hot cup of Folgers Coffee, droning on about how President Rutherford B. Hayes established Fort Belknap by Executive Order in October, 1855. She boasted that the order was signed by the Great White Fathers on July 3, 1873; the white man's Independence Day and the beginning of our generational Lakota poverty. It was a day of deep sorrow when the Fort Laramie treaties were signed, and the U.S. Government established the wildlife Indian reserves across all of the Lakota homelands. The Fort Belknap reservation became just another ghostly reminder of broken spirits and shattered hearts for those who survived. During the great genocide, the U.S. Government named all of the outposts after the now famous white men who killed the most Indians.

Mary Jane, First Holy Woman, was lost to her people in the Dakota Territories and denied her culture according to the U.S. Government federal policy. She spent the rest of her life trying to retrieve her identity back from the U.S. Government. It was as if she was being punished for taking up with one of the white eyes. She was no longer a part of her native family and yet did not exist to his Pennsylvania blue blood family. Mary Jane made dozens of trips from Lodge Pole to Wolf Point trying to get her pedigree papers from the War Department. They made promises that she would one day be accepted by the Great White Father and get 'lots of money' from the U.S. Government. Great Grandmother Mary Jane, my grandmother, Julia, and my mother, Mayme, waited their entire lives for the U.S. Government to keep their promise, and they never did.

Bartholomew and Mary Jane tried to earn a living at the turn of the 20th Century running the general store at Lodge Pole. Lodge

Pole was the reservation outpost mostly occupied by Gros Ventre families, and the nearby town of Hays was home to the Assiniboine communities at the southern end of the reservation. They shared poverty, disease, defeat and emotional subjugation by the white hoards flooding the prairie; their autonomous lifestyle now a post traumatic memory. While Bartholomew sold mercantile out the front door; he was aware Mary Jane was giving the merchandise away out the back door to the poorest of the White Clay and Nakoda families. They were starving and could not afford to pay for food. She did not see tribal distinction, only people who were suffering, friends that had come to her for help when they were most in need.

The Indian nations were beaten one by one, the U.S. Government attempted to civilize the remaining few. The children were taken from their homes by the insurgent white terrorists and sent to far-away places like Carlyle, Pennsylvania, near Bartholomew's hometown. Later they were sent to Pierre, South Dakota, or Flandreau and Laurence, Kansas, to teach them how to live in the white world. They were taught to appreciate literature of the white classics and taught to paint on canvas rather than on buffalo skins. Those who refused the white civilization were forced into generational internment of the reservations. You still hear the drums of the modern resistance, but the diabetic chemical warfare persists across the nations. Alcoholism rates are flooded with the residual toxins of methamphetamine grief.

The White Clay and Nakoda, like the survivors of other reservations, never recovered from the genocide. The irony remains that many of these people treat each other as badly as the U.S. War Department treated them at the turn of the century. There are rich and poor White Clay and Nakoda people depending on their cunning and greed. Success is determined by the fall count of the tribal council ballots and post-election results. The White

Clay or A'aninin people were cousins of the fiercest of the Blackfeet Confederacy and Nakoda Nation. The U.S. Government took all the Indian land away by force, even the homelands in the Dakota Territories were gone, given to the settlers for the taking of Lakota scalps and a .30 Remington slug.

When the buffalo vanished from the prairie and the prairie grass was turned to sod, so went the warriors' ways of Lakota socialism and caring for the weak and helpless. The U.S. Government confiscated our traditional Lakota ghost shirts and we were taught to be white, just like them. We were taught the skill of Coyote drinking, seeking excess in the alcohol poison, the toxic darkness that fell, dousing the light of hope in the humanity that once made us men. Alcohol has become the honorary tribal member that makes us cheat and lie for the numbness of our pain. The U.S. Government corrupted our ceremonial peyote spirit visions and the spiritual use of pegi', convincing us that it was evil and that alcohol would cleanse our spirits. That sly Coyote always the lurking trickster, thief and deceitful clown. Our ancestors used him in their stories telling us, beware the path for the coyote tracks behind you. Somehow they didn't see him in the Lager Beer.

Bartholomew and Mary Jane, First Holy Woman, lived among the White Clay and the Nakoda aka Assiniboine people in north-central Montana. They made their home in the Little Rocky Mountains in the midst of the Indian Wars. The White Clay and the Nakoda were resigned to subjugation and settled on the reservation enduring starvation with no way to hunt the remaining wild game scattered across the silent prairie. The White Clay and Nakoda were two different people, now intermarrying, bearing children of mixed breeds. The future brought the certain destruction of both cultures. There would be no more White Clay or Nakoda, and with that the pride and tenacity would go with it. For Bartholomew, civilization came easy and was familiar; for

Mary Jane this change was as foreign as her name. They lived in a log house and First Holy Woman learned a whole new way of cooking on a cast iron stove. The change was slow; it took adjustment and leaving behind her culture, and with it, her beliefs. White civilization, the White Clay, and the Nakoda were all so foreign to this Lakota woman. She had to learn their ways to survive.

The White Clay had some peculiar beliefs. They believe they are made of the clay found along the river bottoms of the Milk River. The French fur trappers and traders brought the alcohol poison, flour and sugar to complete the great equation. The genocide encroached at an insidious gradual pace, crawling at the edge of time so nobody noticed. The French greedily traded the alcohol poison for unlimited furs and women. They took the wealth of the White Clay in a hearty exchange for the new honorary tribal member that spoke in Coyote language, the homemade distillation of all Indian grief.

The Nakoda's cousins, the A'ananin, were separated years before by the trail of the buffalo and the quest for a warrior's adventure following the legend of the 'Trickster'. They followed the herds and harvested the native fruits, choke cherries, golden currents and elderberries of the North American plains. They hunted elk, deer and mountain sheep for pemmican and dried strips of meat for sustenance in the winter camps.

The White Clay people wintered among the pines and aspens near Chief Mountain in peaceful coexistence among the fierce Blackfeet nations. The Nakoda pursued the ancient buffalo herds who called to them in their dreams...*Follow the life source for growth and survival*...or submit to entropic collapse and destruction if you should stop moving. They were separated from their homeostatic coexistence with the Lakota Yankton people for a 'thousand moons' following the herds, so the legend goes. The Nakoda followed the buffalo by listening to the wind, the voice of Itate', which provided them guidance. The buffalo herds provided all that was needed to live as honorable and respected 'human beings'. They contributed to the tribal food supply for sustenance and hides for warmth from the Montana-Dakota winters. The buffalo hide tee-pees accommodated the home-fire camps, and the 'talking circles' of the tribal council's discussions and its decision making. These were all gifts from Wakan Tanka, also known as the Great Mystery.

The buffalo were the measure of Indian prosperity for the plains tribes. The last remnants of the wild herds, now U.S. Government buffalo, remained in the Bear Paw and Little Rocky Mountains, amidst the lush grasses of the Milk River Valley of the White Clay and the Nakoda. When all the buffalo were gone and there was nothing left to kill, the U.S. Government was war weary. Their institutional wisdom devised a social control policy which effectively maintained tribal entropic decline that is still today defined by poverty rates, domestic violence, drug, and alcohol addictions. They put natural tribal enemies together on the wild Indian reserves hoping they would kill each other off. The White Clay and the Nakoda are still fighting like packs of wild dogs, both parties hoping for the pittance and 'bones' of U.S. Government Federal Register allocations.

Uncle Boots, Uncle Tommy and my dad sat around the round oak table drinking Lucky Lager beer and sipping from a fifth of Seagram's 7 debating; sounding more like an argument with every tip of the bottle. Uncle Boots was the oldest and remembered the stories Bartholomew and Mary Jane told when they were young. Every Indian story is a sad story. Being a 'half-breed' was no easy task in those days; it's no easy task no matter what day it is. Back then you knew where you stood, the only good Indian was a dead

Indian. That's just the way it was. Now-a-days, they just put up civilized signs, 'no dogs or Indians allowed'. Drinking late into the evening, with KOJM a.m. radio droning in the background, the stories weaved my childish understanding of where I came from and who my ancestors were. There wasn't much to be proud of being an Indian in 1958; being Indian was little more than being human. It wasn't until the 70's when 'the wannabees' after the movie *Soldier Blue* about the Sand Creek Massacre made it a fad to be Native American. If it weren't for Peter Strauss and Candice Bergen, we might still be living in teepees.

It was springtime in the Black Hills and the earth was alive and rushing toward summer bloom in 1831 when my great uncle Tatanka Íyotake was born. The white expansion had already begun by 1776 when the patriots crafted the U.S. Constitution. It was the white man's declaration by the rich people and especially for the rich. The federal government took the liberty of giving all of the Indian land away to foreigners who could not speak our language.

Sitting Bull's fate was sealed years before his birth, his future predetermined. He became a Húŋkpapȟa, meaning head of a circle, a Lakota holy man, not by choice, but by destiny and defiance. He led his people through the desert like a Native American Moses during the oppositional defiant Lakota resistance to the federal Indian policies. Tatanka Íyotake shared the council fires and spoke increasing words from the prophecy of the Ghost Dance throughout the Dakota Territories. Before the Battle of the Little Bighorn, Sitting Bull told the council of his Ghost Dance vision. He saw the defeat of the 7th Calvary and General Custer in the polarizing future. His medicine man vision gave the Lakota the spirit, determination and the will to defeat the 7th Calvary.

Sitting Bull was unaware that this was the 'beginning of the end' for the Lakota. The cultural self-determination, self-autonomy and authentic self was at stake and the outcome was calculated. With desperation they turned to the Ghost Dance and a man of peace named Jack Wilson. He was a Paiute 'half-breed' known as Wovoka among the people. The half-breed took the Ghost Dance prophecy to the tribes in the southwest and brought the ceremony back in 1859. The Wovoka teachings espoused that an Indian must live 'in a good way' and resist the alcohol demon if they were to eradicate the evils of the white man. The U.S. Government feared the spiritual Ghost Dance that inspired the stubborn oppositional defiant Lakota resistance to the great American genocide. The ceremony prophesized the eradication of government control over the Lakota people. The prophecy guided them to join the resistance through civil disobedience in the years to come.

The spiritual origin of the Ghost Dance was an ancient ceremony used by many Indian 'human beings' since the ongoing hordes of white invaders arrived on our native shores. All of the people across the Indian landscape assimilated the ancient rituals into their own spiritual beliefs. Sitting Bull said it would guarantee success at the Little Big Horn, and it did. It is said that Sitting Bull was murdered by the U.S. Government insurgency at the Standing Rock Indian Reservation during an attempt to silence him following the Indian wars. The reason for their suspicion was the U.S. Government's fear of the Lakota Ghost Dance and the power that came with it. Even more they feared the growing Ghost Dance beliefs and power among the southwest tribes. It was predestined that Sitting Bull would die on December 15, 1890, and that his spirit would manifest itself in my life in my fourth year.

Tshunke Witco, known as Crazy Horse, took up arms against the U.S. Government to fight their encroachment into the Dakota Territories. He led the Lakota, Cheyenne and Arapaho 'cousins' in the Battle of the Little Bighorn in June, 1876. After surrendering to the U.S. Calvary in 1877, he and his band of Oglala Lakota were 'marched' 40 miles from Camp Sheridan to surrender to General Crook at the Red Cloud Agency on Sunday, May 6, 1877. Tshunke Witco was fatally wounded that same year on September 5 by a Lakota outcast U.S. Calvary soldier. It was claimed that he was resisting the Auschwitz-Dachau internment at Camp Robinson in the Nebraska Territories. Crazy Horse was the most noble of war chiefs and he is now interred in stone. Crazy Horse's family, shadowed in grief, took his body for secret burial in a high meadow in the Black Hills. His brother Little Hawk said he arose three days later and ascended with the eagles and the hawks to the sky.

Black Elk, a cousin of Tshunke Witco, recalled, 'When I was a man, my father told me something about Crazy Horse's vision.' Of course he did not know all of it, but he said that Crazy Horse dreamed and went into the world where there is nothing but the spirits of all things. That is the real world that is behind this one, and everything we see here is something like a shadow from that reality. In that world, he, the horse he rode, the trees and the grass and the stones and everything were made of spirit, and nothing was hard; everything seemed to float. His horse was stood still there, and yet it danced around like a horse made only of shadow. That is how he got his name, which does not mean that his horse was crazy or wild, but that in his vision it danced around in a strange way… it was this vision that gave him his great power, for when he went into a fight, he had only to think of that world to be in it again, so that he could go through anything and not be hurt. Until he was killed at the soldiers' town on the White River, Tshunke Witko was wounded only twice in his lifetime, once by accident, and each time by one of his own people when he was not expecting trouble and was not thinking, never by an enemy.

Chapter 3

Biodynamic Infestations of Shame and Despair

Victor and I were playing in the tractor tire sandbox that was outside the dilapidated shed door at the entryway to our five room mansion. I heard a car pulling in the long driveway. The splash of the tires in the mud puddle gave warning. The '38 Ford rounded the corner with the radiator boiling over; it was my mom's brothers, Uncle Dempsey and Uncle Jerry.

Jerry was driving and both were drunker than skunks. Uncle Jerry gave Victor and me each a shiny quarter, bending over to find out what we were doing playing in the dirt. He almost fell into the sandbox. I smelled the mixture of alcohol and shaving lotion on his clean shaven face. My mother came out to welcome them, as they boisterously greeted their sister with a dancing Lakota bear hug. Uncle Dempsey dropped his box of Lucky Lager bottles on the ground. We helped him gather his bottles of liquid insanity as he staggered into the house.

My dad was home recovering from a night of World War II trauma drinking at Kennedy's Bar with Ralph Modic and closed mouth vets. They shared games of pinochle and Seagram's 7 memories. Uncle Dempsey offered him a Lucky Lager, he nodded his head yes and grinned his blue eyed leprechaun grin. He searched for the 'church key' bottle opener. Uncle Jerry and Dempsey argued about the old homestead they had just come from, searching for pieces of their forgotten history. Victor and I sat silently; the rhythm of drinking had started and there was no stopping it until that box of Lucky Lager vanished before our eyes. My mother scolded her brothers for their pitiful presentation and obvious binge with the devil at their heels. Coyote was waiting around the corner to lead them astray, as always. Both Dempsey and Jerry were World War II veterans, Dempsey at Pearl Harbor and Jerry in the Philippines. It was peculiar how they relived the Indian Wars and memories of their grandparents. The stories got louder as the pile of empty bottles grew. The post trauma of the previous generation seemed to heal their own scars, wounds and nightmares. As the depth of my understanding grew, so did the burden of telling their stories; evasion on this day, like most conversations turned to Little Big Horn.

Not all Indians are to be trusted. The Crow were well known as 'back-stabbers' among other tribes. They had a long history of a two-faced friendship with the arrogant U.S. Calvary who professed a divine right to the blood stained prairie left in their wagon tracks. They traded with the stream of westward homesteaders; the passage of time became a means of gaining favor with their enemy. Their prophecies told the Crow if they helped the 'Son of the Morning Star', the one called Custer, target the military strike against the Lakota, Cheyenne and Arapahoe; the Crow would be spared from certain annihilation. The curse the Crow set on themselves was never removed. The Lakota's inherent bias and visceral genetic predisposition of mistrust of the Crow tribe was forever. The

Lakota and Crow's mistrust is parallel to the perspective of the Jewish-Israeli people towards historical Nazi Germany or the Palestinian Authority.

Victor and I sat in the corner listening intently. Victor's eyes grew wider as he listened to the stories for the first time. I'd heard them over and over. "Is that true?" he asked. "I guess so," I said, "They talk about it every time they drink…like it was yesterday… like Sitting Bull and Crazy Horse are still fighting the battle… besides, they lost…John Wayne and Audie Murphy are my heroes." We were drawn back to the story with the simultaneous popping of bottle tops with church keys. The Battle of the Little Bighorn was a brutal fight to the death engagement for Custer as his thirst for blood rose to a frenzy. The U.S. Government and the Great White Father intended for the total decimation of the Lakota, the genocide of the 'human beings' and all Indian humanity. This time all of the 'human beings' heard the voices of the Ghost Dance spirits to guide their Lakota justice. The combined Lakota, Cheyenne and Arapahoe nations gathered in what they called the 'valley of the greasy grass' to fight for their homelands.

For a short man, Uncle Dempsey sat tall in the saddle as he told his version of the battle he had heard from his Gramma Mary Jane. She heard it from the lips of Gall, Sitting Bull and Crazy Horse himself. All three nodded their heads in agreement, they'd all heard the same story from Gramma Cooshie, and she never lied. As it was told, the battle of the Little Big Horn was indeed Custer's last stand and the day of his reckoning with the devil Coyote near the Yellowstone in the Montana Territories. Crazy Horse by then was a great war chief of the Lakota. He gave the war cry that sent Custer to his deceitful death in the hot Montana prairie sun. Custer died because he did not listen to the Lakota 'speak'. Their prophecy told of his impending death during the summer moon if he did not listen. In the end, his body lay there, both of his ears stabbed and punctured with an elk bone awl so he would listen to the Lakota in the next world. It was an overwhelming victory for the Lakota, Northern Cheyenne and Arapahoe who had joined together in the spirit.

Sitting Bull's certainty of his vision, the Lakota belief in the ancestral Ghost Dance spirits, defeated Custer's cavalry battalion of 700 men. Five of the 7th Cavalry's companies were annihilated in retribution for the progressive Indian genocide across the nations. The peoples' anger was spoken with every strike of their war clubs and thrust of their lances. The Lakota had been antagonized for long enough and in one explosive response asserted their pent up revenge. Custer was killed without grace in sacred defeat by the Lakota, Cheyenne, and Arapahoe 'cousins'. Custer paid for his genocidal sins along with his two brothers, a nephew, and brother -in-law. The battle lasted for the two-day Lakota oppositional defiant outrage against the U.S. Government's manifest destiny determination. The memories will last a hundred generations…until the color white turns to brown.

To escape certain capture, Sitting Bull and his band left the Montana Territories for the Wood Mountain in Saskatchewan, Canada. There they found refuge in the cold northern winters along the Milk River, hunting the sparse game for their winter camps. Sitting Bull had become friends with a 'Wasi'chu' named James Walsh of the North-West Mounted Police. They shared campfires, pipes and puppy feasts when game was scarce. Wasi'chu takes the fat or is a greedy white person traditionally, but in the modern Indian movement, Wasi'chu now means the corporations and rich, with their governmental accomplices that continue to want Indians' lives, land and their resources for their own profit.

Walsh was sympathetic to the Lakota. He was the assigned area commanding officer during Sitting Bull's exile in Canada. It was rumored by some that Walsh was part Indian and had children in the nations. This friendship evolved into genuine expression of the 'low context' verbal extreme European communication; Walsh loved to talk and always asked questions.

Sitting Bull answered in a fully expressive 'high context' style with a grunt and 'pointing of the lips'. Most important, this friendship assured the safety and protection of his Lakota family during their forced stay in the Canadian Territories. He remained in Canada until 1881 when he remorsefully surrendered to the U.S. Calvary.

Gall, a war leader in his own right and one of Tatanka Íyotake's followers, survived many battles during the great genocide. In June, 1876, he rode his war pony with Crazy Horse at the Little Big Horn. Following the battle, he regrouped his surviving warriors in the Yellowstone Valley and headed north. They were unprepared for the long journey; they went with their victory and their wounds. Game was scarce, and campfires were considered risky and sure for capture. Gall led the remaining Húŋkpapȟa bands through the Missouri River, through the White Clay and Nakoda hunting grounds. They escaped to Canada to join Sitting Bull and winter in the Northern Rocky Mountains in an area where the rivers travel in three directions, called Triple Divide. They followed the seasons and herds to the Saskatchewan Valley along the White Clay Peoples' Milk River birthplace in Canada.

The Montana Territories were under siege in the 1870's with the ongoing genocide and the recent defeat and annihilation of the fierce Nez Perce nations. The Lakota resistance at the Little Big Horn, and the humiliation of the Great White Father's narcissistic failures only spurred the U.S. Calvary on with hatred and anger for the 'red man'. There was no refuge for the Lakota, Cheyenne or the Arapahoe. They were sought out with all of the military might that the U.S. Government could muster.

With fear in the air, Bartholomew and Mary Jane were not safe from the bloody anger of the Great White Father or the mistaken wrath on all 'human beings'. Bartholomew was considered a 'squaw-man' and both he and Mary Jane were targets for the white world. For the sympathy he showed to the Lakota and for her being Lakota, they were easy marks for both the white insurgents and the raiding war parties. The mortally wounded spirit of the indigenous people was driven by the Ghost Dance vision of Tatanka Íyotake. The belief and hope in its power grew temporarily with the prophecy of Wovoka.

Bartholomew and Mary Jane found shelter at Fort Buford in the Dakota Territories. He worked as a blacksmith for the cavalry, sweating at the forge over blazing iron and the blast of army bellows. Mary Jane learned the white man ways, cleaning and cooking, baking bread and canning wild choke cherries, raspberries and dried prickly pear cactus. They hunkered down in spite of the 'squaw-man' taunts and the humiliation that Mary Jane faced from the women at the fort. Bartholomew's contact with his family in Pennsylvania became less and less frequent in spite of his mother's worry. The surrounding devastation throughout the Lakota nations came by dispatch, and settlers wounded in sporadic raids spread cataclysmic hate and fear among the outposts, sharing their fear of the bloodthirsty savages that had overwhelmed them in the savage dawn. My great uncle William was born at Fort Buford in the summer heat of July, 1873, as the Ball family continued to make their way westward to the Montana Territories. Great Uncle William was to become my grandfather 76 years later.

The smell of frybread and bean soup wafted through the room. "C'mon you guys, you better sit up and get something to eat," my mother said with authority. "You best sober up and get something in your stomach." Dempsey grunted, "Ughhh...food will ruin our jag!" They moved in synchronized motion, slightly wobbling from effects of the Lucky Lager. "C'mon Victor, let's get some frybread and soup," I asserted, growing tired of the same old stories repeated as if repetition could change the way things were. We learned our place in poverty; we lived on the Northside with the rest of the poor people on our block. It was all we knew. Victor told me stories of people he knew with indoor toilets and bathtubs in their own rooms. We shit in an old outhouse and bathed in the big washtub in the living room. I often wondered why Victor hung out with me listening to all these stories. I heard them so often I could repeat them in my sleep. He was fascinated that we were actually related to these great men of history. I only saw them as losers. John Wayne was the real winner and my hero!

The genocide of the late 19th Century heated up. The Lakota, the Cheyenne and Arapahoe shared conferential beliefs. They had lost their spirit in a post-traumatic retreat from the U.S. Calvary's westward manifest destiny expansion. Wovoka and the Ghost Dance brought Sitting Bull hope. Bartholomew and Mary Jane found their way along the Missouri River trail across the Montana Territories. It was 'Indian Summer' as they made their way in the growing cold, finding sustenance on scarce deer, antelope, and rabbit stew. The buffalo were rapidly disappearing; the small scattered herds spread sparsely across the western plains. Mary Jane was nearing delivery of her second child when they arrived at the Wolf Point outpost near Fort Peck Agency. My grandmother, Julia, was born in a blizzard in December, 1874 at the outpost. They spent the winter at Wolf Point as the genocide continued to escalate. Mary Jane's Lakota family asserted their Ghost Dance ego strength and confidently talked of war as the battle cries grew stronger.

Bartholomew continued to earn a meager living in Wolf Point with his horseshoeing trade and by hunting wild game. His frustrations built and his drinking escalated along with kicking the dog. Mary Jane gathered the harvest of the land, the wild current berries, elderberries and thimbleberries, as they retreated from the war. The U.S. Calvary systematically eliminated the instigators of the Ghost Dance movement from the Mississippi River, the Great Plains, and westward across the Rocky Mountains…to the home of Chief Seattle on the west coast, where dance was outlawed by fearful white authorities. With the growing unrest in the Montana Territories; those who participated in the dance and their children became the embodiment for the hatred of Sitting Bull, Crazy Horse and cousin Gall. As tensions rose, Bartholomew again retreated back to the safety of Fort Buford in the Dakota Territories. My great aunt, Josephine, was born during a wet snow blizzard of the hard spring thaw of April, 1876.

Bartholomew, with the responsibility of his Lakota wife and three children, hesitantly returned to his Pennsylvania home to bury his father in the Fall of 1885, filled with fatigue and with a saddened heavy heart. He told his foreign stories about the civilized Lakota, Northern Cheyenne and the Arapahoe and his adventures in the Dakota and Montana Territories. He cautiously introduced his family to his non-English speaking Lakota wife, Mary Jane, and his 'half breed' children. His younger sister, Katherine 'Katie' Ball, begged him not to return west to the Dakota Territories. She cried in fear for his life and the ongoing uncertainty in Dakota and Montana. Bartholomew's family refused to accept his wife or the children, but with Mary Jane and the children safe in Pennsylvania, they managed to stay for one long year. The treatment of his children in the white schools in Carlyle finally drove him to return to the Dakotas. He and First Holy Woman made the 1,500-mile journey with their children and continued westward from the Dakotas towards the mountains with hopes of finding acceptance in the post-traumatic, war-torn west. With his family's savage shame, they traveled and Bartholomew returned them to Fort Buford.

Out in the Montana Territories the hunt for Chief Joseph, Hinmatóowyalahtq'it, ended at Fort Assiniboine. Chief Joseph was the leader of the Nez Perce from the Wallowa Valley in northeastern Oregon. The U.S. Government gave away the Nez Perce land to the white settlers who came for gold. They came in swarms of greed, like the summer locust migrations. Chief Joseph and Chief Looking Glass led their band of Oregon Nez Perce who had been forcibly moved to Idaho for 1,200 miles across Idaho and Wyoming. Their only chance at survival was to join Sitting Bull in Canada, and the newspapers dubbed their fighting retreat as the Nez Perce War. Finally, Joseph and his people met their demise only 40 miles from the Canadian border in northcentral Montana. General Howard's horse soldiers were angered and enraged by the Nez Perce defectors. Chief Joseph's band had brought their Palouse tribal allies from the Wallowa Valley to the far away Montana prairie to die at 'Ca'ynun-a-wka-spe'…meaning the place of manure in the winter of 1877. The white insurgent terrorist government soldiers were led by Cheyenne and Lakota traitors in the pursuit of the Nez Perce renegades. Soldiers terrorized the settlers along the way, with threats of death if they refused to help find the fleeing band of Nez Perce elders, women and children.

With Bartholomew's unspoken rejection of his white privilege, he and Mary Jane left Fort Buford with their three 'half-breed' children traveling in an 1862 government issue Conestoga wagon. It was filled with meager household goods, horseshoeing tools, forge and bellows. It was brimming with renewed hope and optimism. They followed the familiar trail along the Missouri River to Wolf Point and onward west to the safety of Fort Assiniboine and the Milk River Valley…the home of the White Clay and the Nakoda. They found temporary relief at the Milk River Agency outpost. They claimed sanctuary at Little Chief Canyon in the Little Rocky Mountains due east of the Fort Assiniboine Agency. Ol' Andrew Whitehorse befriended them and helped them through the first hard Montana Territory winter. My great uncle, Thomas, was born in July, 1878, at the Milk River outpost at Fort Assiniboine.

There was a devastating drought that year across the Dakota and Montana Territories. Farmers and newcomers suffered dearly; most of the crops and cattle died of thirst.

After the government took the Nez Perce land, it was rumored they were promised a 'lot of money' in treaty settlements. The bloodstained U.S. Government authoritarian bureaucrats built schools to save the Indian from his own primitive pagan ways. White Catholic priests and school matrons beat the Indian out of their students' Nez Perce hearts while praying for their lost souls. The government built band-aid hospitals to heal the broken bones of the Nez Perce women. The broken bones were a displaced post-traumatic anger meant for the Great White Father's genocidal humanity. "I shall fight no more..." echoed across the Palouse Valley; Chief Joseph and 400 warriors of the Nez Perce and Palouse were held in captivity by the white insurgency. First loaded into railroad cattle cars and hauled to the frozen Kansas internment camps at Fort Leavenworth, they were moved again by icy steel rail to the Auschwitz and Dachau camps in the Oklahoma Hills. Warriors took their captive anger out on their women and children. Most of the Nez Perce resistance died of the humiliation.

The genocide ended with the Wounded Knee Massacre in the 1890's and the death of Spotted Elk on December 29, 1890, near 'Chankpe' O'pi Wakpala' on the Lakota Pine Ridge Reservation in the South Dakota Territories. At last the Lakota, Northern Cheyenne and Arapahoe were worn from fatigue and weary from their tears, grief and failure. They were cast into a future of generational despair, poverty and a history of loss. The terrorist insurgency destroyed the paramount nomadic co-existence of all the nations. The white man's greed for land, guaranteeing generations of post-traumatic stress disorders, shameless anti-social personality disorders, domestic violence, alcoholism and loss of ego function for the Indian nations. They gave away their self-worth, self-respect and self-esteem while following the Trickster's deceit, lies and the Great White Father's broken promises.

The day before the massacre at Wounded Knee, a detachment of the U.S. 7th Cavalry Regiment under the command of Major Samuel M. Whitside captured Spotted Elk's band of Miniconjou Lakota and 38 Hunkpapa Lakota warriors near Porcupine Butte. These defeated and captured warriors were escorted five miles west to Chankpe' O'pi Wakpala where they made camp. The remainder of the 7th Calvary Regiment arrived, led by Colonel James Forsyth, and strategically surrounded the Lakota encampment. The U.S. Calvary 'weapons of mass destruction' were assembled and the four Hotchkiss Gatling guns were directed on the Lakota encampment. On the morning of December 29, the soldiers rode into the Lakota Wounded Knee encampment. A deaf Lakota elder named Black Coyote was reluctant to give up his hunting rifle, claiming he had paid two horses for it. There was a chaotic Lakota scuffle and the 7th Cavalry indiscriminately opened fire from the four holy directions, killing men, women and children.

By the time the teepees had burned, the military effort had achieved near total destruction and annihilation of all the Lakota people at Wounded Knee Creek that day. Black Coyote was left to bleed to death in freezing waters, washing his spirit back to the earth. The razor swords of the U.S. Cavalry soldiers' bloody steel silenced the heartbeats of elders, men, women and children… all dead in the bloody frozen snow. As the smoke cleared and the burning lodges smoldered in the morning sun, the moans could be heard of the wounded that never saw the next Lakota sunset. Three hundred scorched souls lost their lives, left frozen, buried in the ground. Soldiers took the remaining men, women and children in handcuffs and leg-irons by freight wagons to the Auschwitz-Dachau internment camps at Fort Sill to beat the pagan devils out of them, fill them with the spirit of Christianity and the goodness of Jesus; a Christian Stockholm syndrome.

You can hear the whispers of Itate' in the four holy winds as they blow across the Dakota Territories. His words haunt descendants with unconscious guilt and shame for the conscious genocide perpetrated by their ancestors. Their ignorance of their white privilege is like a stain that will never wash from the white man's soul. The ancient spirit of the Ghost Dance blanketed the Great White Father's manifest destiny narcissism in the broken burning rubble of authoritarian bureaucratic institutional glass and steel of modern day terrorist attacks. " How could they do this to us…why do they hate us this much?" the white man asks. White superiority is blind to the benefit of the privileges they have bestowed on themselves. In 1890 The Great White Fathers honored the U.S. Calvary for a job well done; gracious medals of honor were awarded for their savage brutality at Wounded Knee.

Only the strongest Viktor Frankl minds of the 'human beings' survived the post trauma of the Indian holocaust; the rest died in the Dachau-Auschwitz internment camps in the Kansas and Oregon Territories. They died of small pox and infectious biodynamic infestations of shame and despair. Although Chief Joseph pled his case for the Nez Perce in 1879 to the Great White Fathers in Washington D.C., he was not allowed to return home for six more years. He struggled with his life's journey and failure until 1904 when he was laid to rest in his happy hunting ground. Wounded Knee was the defining signature of the U.S. Government's genocidal humanity; it was the most horrific of their Indian campaigns. They assassinated at least 153 Lakota elder men, woman and children in the freezing Dakota winter. The Indian wars left the native nations in post-traumatic grief, displacement of cultures and stripped of identities. The victims were blamed for their failures and white supremacy ruled the outcomes.

Chapter 4

Precursory Arrival in This Ambivalent World

There wasn't much to do in our five room mansion during the dreary winters on the Montana Hi-Line, the ribbon of Highway 2 that cuts across the northern-most tier of the Montana prairie. The Dearborn gas heater blazed in a never ending struggle against the howling wind and the Milk River freeze. Our house was refuge for relatives down on their luck, recovering from a binge of Coyote drinking or hiding from their women. My cousins stayed with us, doing nothing to arouse the chill, drinking boiling hot coffee and playing cards. I learned from them the art of being an Indian, grunting and pointing with my lips. My mother sat at the oak table, drinking her scalding hot Lipton tea, although there was always a pot of Folger's coffee warming on the heater in the living room. It really wasn't a living room, just the room in the center of the five room mansion big enough for the oak table. We all sort of gravitated to the table and bench stools at supper time. The red beans and bacon soup, fried potatoes and fresh side pork was a feast of Indian soul food. The smell of fresh homemade biscuits made the meal complete.

The relatives told the stories from their childhood, all reminding me how good I had it in this day of modern convenience and running water. Things hadn't always been this modern; it was the '60's and the government took care of our people. Paradoxically, sometime in the 1880's, the U.S. Government built the hospital at Fort Belknap where they tried to save the White Clay and Nakoda from the white man diseases they brought to the nations. It was commonly know across the nations that IHS was an ongoing experimentation and we were their training ground. The huge three-story brick hospital building was at the end of the long driveway off of U.S. Highway 2 just east of the Milk River bridge. It remains as an icon of the Great White Father's authoritarian bureaucratic institutional control, filled with the cure for the post-traumatic stress disorders of the holocaust. In Bartholomew and Mary Jane's time, the hospital ride from Ball's Canyon was two to three days by buck board wagon, depending on the weather and occasional flash floods. The Indian people learned to suffer in silence, mostly continuing the traditional practices.

By the turn of the 20th Century, the reservation was well infested with diseased alcoholic thought, its people stunned with post traumatic grief and a voracious thirst for the white man's spiritual medication. There was an epidemic of idiopathic broken dreams, diffuse loss of skeletal backbone and warrior's spine. The 12-bed hospital could only repair the broken bones but not the fractured souls; government doctors took little care to fix the bullet holes and stab wounds inflicted in the growing alcohol-washed despair. I was born at Fort Belknap Hospital not many years ago. I swear I can remember the oxygen tent I lived in the first months of my life. I lay in confinement, unable to touch my mother, unable to experience human touch, the groundwork laid for critical impingement and oppositional defiant trust issues with the external world. The barrier prevented me from getting too close; looking out I could see the worry on my mother's face. She touched the glass barrier with her finger tips; my heart pounded on the glass in despair.

My mother went about the task of baking bread, ten loaves, four pans of homemade biscuits and two dishpans of frybread at a time. It was an all-day task as she talked on about Great Grandfather Bartholomew's sister. "She came to visit him at Lodge Pole. She was a grand white lady from back east in Pennsylvania. Her name was Katherine our Aunt Katie Sweeny. She drove a Model T and was an independent woman of means. She wore a hat with all kinds of fancy colored feathers. I have a picture of her in my picture box…you seen it I'm sure. Hershey, I think it was… Hershey, Pennsylvania. Anyway, she came to visit her big brother Bartholomew." My mother reminisced, "I was five years old when I met her… Aunt Katie…her and Mr. Hershey her intended. He was from way back east too. She sure was a high class magnificent lady, n'it'. They didn't stay long though…Grampa didn't know why. They were here a few days and then they left again. I was seven when we learned she died and went to the 'white man' heaven in a fancy garden. Grampa was sad but he couldn't cry."

Aunt Katie died when she was 42 years old of a terrible "Hunting" (Huntington's) disease; my mom, Mayme, met her Aunt Katie and Mr. Hershey just that once. The news arrived after the funeral that she had passed away. Bartholomew never said a word, just looked out over the valley in silence. Mary Jane knew he needed his peace and went silently about taking care of the kids and the ranch chores for fear of his drinking and anger. The letters from home were sparse as the old folks passed on one by one. Only a few childhood relatives kept in contact. Letters took a month to reach Lodge Pole from Pennsylvania. There never seemed to be a time Bartholomew was not needed on the ranch. The stock needed tending, hay needed cutting, the fall roundup and herding stock to market was a full time job, not to mention gathering the winter wood supply. The seamless transition of the seasons kept his forgotten world of Pennsylvania separate from his new life with Mary Jane and their family. Within a couple generations he was forgotten in Pennsylvania, just a faded name in the family bible of an uncle who went west, never to return.

My mother's stories about my great grandmother First Holy Woman, 'Cooshie,' are burned in our memories. It was curious how both my mother and father talked of her with reverent natal affection. The stories they shared of her at Devil's Lake, playing on the prairie with her cousin Gall and hiding from the soldiers; even the story my parents told of First Holy Woman being stolen by her future husband, and her father, Itate', seeking vengeance on Bartholomew implied a shared heritage. There was an unspoken truth...my Grandfather William and Grandmother Julia were brother and sister. Over time, I understood this with unconscious intuition.

My grandmother, Julia Ball, was born in 1874. She was born in a two room shack in the Milk River Valley, an Indian shack in what we know as 'Little Chicago'. The black buffalo soldiers had lived there during the genocide, and they vacated with the Indian holocaust. I listened to my mother tell the stories of how hard life was for her mother, Julia, and Mom's aunt and uncles, William, Josephine and Thomas, growing up as 'half-breed' Lakota. It was a world of white privilege which brought with it the White Clay and Nakoda mistrust of her 'half-breed' precursory arrival in this ambivalent world.

Julia Ball was 14 years old in 1888 when the U.S. Government reorganized the Fort Assiniboine installation, establishing the

Fort Belknap Reservation; and in so doing, taking the land Bartholomew Ball's family homesteaded on. They deeded the land to the Montana Territories and distributed it to the land barons and people of power. History books have been written about the corruption of the honkytonk towns and the whore houses that came with the Burlington Northern Railroad during the civilization of Hill and Blaine counties. The rapes and murders of Indian women, left to die in white supremacist cum-stained clothes; they were perceived as less than human, less than the white whores that worked the brothels. The Fort Belknap Indian Reservation served to maintain control of the White Clay and Nakoda. Bartholomew and Mary Jane's original homestead was now centered at the south-end of the newly sanctioned reservation. They were safer there than off the reservation; the law of the land was dangerous for Indians who strayed near drunken white men with guns. The Ball family's property was no longer theirs, but Mary Jane and Bartholomew were given permission to stay on the homestead at Ball's Canyon until their death.

The Montana Territories were filled with danger, not only from the scourge of war, but from entertainment of the white bank robbers, train robbers and highwaymen. Harvey Logan was a young drifter and drover who came to the territory with his brothers. They started a ranch near Ball's Canyon, across the mountain, over Monument Peak near the gold mining town of Landusky. One night at the Landusky Saloon, drifter Harvey Logan came to deadly terms with Pike Landusky, namesake of the town and saloon. Harvey feared for his life, let 'no moss grow' and headed south to the Colorado Territory. Sometime later Logan, now known as 'Kid Curry', returned to Montana and the Logan family ranch. Curry and his gang frequented the Ball homestead, where Bartholomew lived out his own young adventurous spirit. Kid Curry seems to have been a welcome guest; Mary Jane and my grandmother, Julia, humorously reminisced about their infatuation with his boyish charm. They laughed and giggled at his childish flirtations. Curry and his rowdy bunch befriended Mr. Bill Allen and his new wife, Julia. Mr. Allen often let them take refuge with the horses and gave them fresh mounts.

Julia cooked for the gang and gave them supplies as they drifted around Phillips County, robbing and raiding the commuter train called "The Caboose" that ran Malta carrying local passengers and bank shipments. The Curry bunch often found themselves on the run from the law. They frequently needed to cross through Ball's Canyon on the way to their hideout in the Little Rockies south of Landusky. The slippery refugees from justice hooked up with Butch Cassidy and the Sundance Kid in Colorado country. They weaved their way, returning to the sagebrush prairie of north central Montana, robbing banks along the trail from Belle Fourche, South Dakota to Minot, North Dakota. They dodged the law, avoiding towns and travelers, and frequently annoyed the Union Pacific Pinkerton detectives with their guerilla style escapes from sure capture. On July 3, 1901, the wild bunch pulled off the biggest Great Northern Railway robbery in history. They disappeared with $41,500 in unsigned legal tender, the biggest news event in all of north-central Montana that year. Everyone alive that year had their version of the robbery and their own heroic deeds. My Uncle Boots was still in a papoose blanket suckin' teat, yet told the most colorful version of the event, all the while drinking his FI Muscatel wine.

My mother, Mayme, never knew her momma Julia's first husband, Colonel William 'Bill' Allen. He was murdered long before she was born. She knew him from the stories she heard from her Mother, Brother John, Aunt Sis and Uncle Boots' memories. She heard them so many times she repeated them verbatim. She told me that my grandmother Julia married Mr. Allen. He was a white colonel in the U.S. Cavalry. He spent many early years during the Indian War campaigns contributing to the genocide of

First Holy Woman's people. He came often to the ranch at Ball's Canyon. It was a holding stage for processing the government cattle allotted to the tribes; he was there to curb the cattle rustling and bring in the rustlers on federal charges. The spark between him and Julia was obvious; he wasn't getting any younger and was looking to settle down. She took extra time, doting over him and seeking him out in the barn to alert his attention. Their affection grew and romance was in bloom. Mr. Allen and Julia were married on January 29, 1891, at Dodson, one year after the Wounded Knee Massacre. The painful irony inherent in these family relationships has left me with a sense of cosmic dissonance and a lifetime of ambivalent confusion…the reality of what my own white-privileged ancestors did to our spiritual self-worth and any chance of cultural self-determination.

Mr. Allen was a U.S. Government 'sub-agent' for the War Department; now it's called the Bureau of Indian Affairs. His job was to scrutinize the government cattle herds designated for tribal distribution to the reservation Indians. In his day these federal beef allocations consisted of 'cattle on the hoof'; in more recent times people came to rely on subsistence sugar and starch-filled government 'commodities' for survival; they inadvertently became the source of the modern diabetic genocide.

The Allen's youngest son, Thomas, was ten years younger than my Aunt Sis. He was often told to ride out and round up strays in the brush up the canyon. On this day Mr. Allen and Julia waited for his return fearing he might be injured. The sun sank quickly in the chilly October evening, then night rolled in. Julia's wailing broke the silence of the early morning. Colonel Allen found his young son beaten, dragged and mutilated, finally shot to death with a .45 slug in his back, his body tied to the gate at Ball's Ranch. It was suspected the killers were from the Colburn ranch, but authorities could never gather substantial proof of their transgressions. You could smell the guilt when they rode by mocking Colonel Allen's government authority as they passed.

Mr. Allen met his fatal demise in a gunfight with his former brother-in-law, Charlie Perry, at the Colburn Ranch in the north-central Montana Territories. My family's version of the story was, 'Mr. Allen, as the federal sub-agent, was attempting to thwart the local ranchers from rustling Indian cattle while the White Clay and Nakoda people starved at the hand of Colburn's white man greed. Eventually all was forgiven because Charlie and his wife, Mary, were the parents of Jeanette Warrior, my mother's cousin through marriage.'

Charlie Perry worked for the Colburn family who had been stealing the White Clay and Nakoda's allotted USDA-approved range cattle. The family story continued, 'It was a brisk spring morning in 1902; Mr. Allen went to the Colburn's *Circle C* ranch on official U.S. Government business. As he walked into the Circle C ranch house, Charlie was standing behind the door and shot Mr. Allen in the back, taking his life as he lay in his own blood on the wood cabin floor.' It was a heated family debate whether Charlie, being a member of the Nakoda tribe, was paid to serve time in prison for the death of Mr. Allen. The irony was Mr. Allen was shot with the pearl handled Colt .44 he had given Charlie for his birthday. This long-argued family legend became the topic of anecdotal humor bound by the friendships between the many descendants of Charlie in a lifetime of the cosmic psychedelic journey.

My great uncle, William Ball, was also my grandfather. It is a confusing and perplexing story and explains much of why I grew up feeling like an outcast. It was also the family secret that everyone knew but me. William married my grandmother, Cecelia Azure, in 1899 at Fort Belknap. She was a Chippewa from Turtle Mountain in the Dakota Territories. Her people had been displaced during the heat of the genocide, and she was born in the fall of 1879 near Great Falls, Montana Territory, in the Cascade Mountains. My great grandparents, Alex and Louise Azure, came west from the Dakota Territories and lived at St. Peter's Mission as the dust settled. They came with the migration of the 'human beings' in 1873, fleeing the manifest destiny of the U.S. Government. The Catholic mission was a safe place for Alex's half-breed wife and children. The anger of the white settlers was still ablaze with their thirst for revenge as hatred grew and festered in the territories.

The Azures found ranch work along the way following the Missouri River Trail; it was the most common and also the most dangerous, especially for breeds. Alex worked for a few days here and there for sympathetic ranchers. He worked mostly for food and shelter 'riding the grub line' as it was called. It was not a matter of pride, but a matter of survival. He also hunted for the meager subsistence game of deer and antelope. There were always prairie chickens and jack rabbits. My great grandmother, Louise, picked choke-cherries and elder-berries along the trail. She made pemmican, a mix of animal fat and berries pounded and stored in three to nine pound rawhide pouches for long term preservation. These high energy bars sustained them in times of little or no game.

Alex and Louise's daughter, Cecelia Azure, went to school at St. Peter's Mission and learned to speak English as her second language. She and William Ball met at a celebration near Lewistown, Montana. It was a sight to see Indians playing fiddles and guitars, drinking and singing in French! Alex Azure and Bartholomew Ball had worked together at Fort Assiniboine back in the old days. William looked for any reason to frequent the Azure camp, and soon he and Cecelia were inseparable. The courtship was a long arduous task before Alex finally gave the couple permission to marry.

Chapter 5

Dempsey vs. Gibbons

The legacy of the genocide left a far reaching imprint on my family. From generation to generation, the post trauma of operational dysfunction grew in an irreparable cycle. It was normal to grow up in such poverty even if you were an Indian. Every Indian story is a sad story. There was nothing expected other than living in chaos, poverty and alcoholic despair. This was the third generation after the genocide. The hatred remained; there was no escape. It was clear that white superiority remained intact as did the barriers to leaving the reservation. It is still true today; those who stay remain dependent on the system that imprisons them. Those who leave are diminished to less than human beings by the white supremacist world. Those who never belonged as enrolled tribal members are driven to the shadows of humanity and left to observe. Those who fight back are abandoned by the ones they are fighting for. The family's claim to Ball's Canyon was worth fighting for; it was the legacy that Bartholomew and Mary Jane First Holy Woman etched out for their children.

After the murder of Mr. William Allen in 1902, my widowed 'half-breed' grandmother, Julia Ball Allen, along with her four 'quarter-breed' children, went back home to live at the ranch at Ball's Canyon with her parents, Bartholomew and Mary Jane. Her kids went to school in Lodge Pole and worked in the fields when they got home. Julia tended the five-acre family garden, growing green beans, tomatoes, squash and corn. She and her children gathered and canned their crops, plus seasonal wild asparagus and berries to last through the winter.

One dusty afternoon a short, hungry rider wandered in looking for water for his horse and a plate of beans to fill his belly. Julia had been widowed for two years, long past the grieving time expected in those days. The philandering drover anticipated he had struck pay-dirt, a widow with aging parents and a ranch complete with children to work it. After a short romance he asked Bartholomew for Julia's hand. Julia wasn't choosey; aware that it would take a strong man to take on a ready-made family. She and George Contway were married on October 23, 1904, in Dodson by Judge Eberschweiler, the local Circuit Court judge. George was 15 years older than Julia; he was a sawed-off runt 'half-breed' Kootenai cowboy born in December, 1859. After the wedding, there was a huge barn dance and celebration at the ranch; all the people from Lodge Pole and even people from across the mountain in Hays and Landusky came.

Years later, my mother, Mayme Contway, went to the back room, the one where she kept her treasures and girlhood mementoes. She came back with a worn Tony Lama cardboard boot box of pictures. There was a photo of my grandparents... George and Julia. I have been told there is a hint of Mexican blood in my eclectic family lineage; maybe George was the source of that rumor. He wore a stovepipe hat like Abe Lincoln to make him look taller. He was quite a bit shorter than my grandmother. She was a tall raw-boned woman with long braided black hair. George came up from the southwest, along the Chisholm Trail from Texas. He had trailed longhorn cattle in the company of a young hard drinkin', cloud watchin' cowboy named Charlie Russell, who was more interested in making pictures than he was in those smelly longhorn critters. George Contway and Charlie parted ways once they got to the Montana Territories. George went north, and Charlie went to 'The Falls'. Great Falls was a thriving railroad town, a city where a fledgling artist could find a start in the land of primitive cultures and memories of buffalo herds across the prairie.

Julia with child and newly married, George took on the foreman duties of running Bartholomew and First Holy Woman's family ranch. He was unaware Ball's Canyon was deeded to the White Clay and Nakoda people upon the deaths of Bartholomew and Mary Jane. George and Julia gave birth to five more 'three eighths-breed' Lakota-Kootenai children with no official tribal affiliation due to First Holy Woman's undocumented Lakota heritage. This assured generations of poverty, a living manifestation and assiduous lineage of *shadow people.* Bartholomew and Mary Jane, now in their 50's, looked back on their journey of the last 30 years. They had survived the holocaust, the chaos and the fear during the Indian Wars. It was time to let their new son-in-law and Julia take over the ranch. They still had many good years to help raise grandkids and watch prairie sunsets. They built a new log home to house their growing family on the homestead.

My uncle, John Allen, was born in 1892, two years after Wounded Knee, and he grew up at Ball's Canyon under the protection of his Grandpa Bartholomew. He was Julia and William Allen's first born and was 12 years old when George Contway married his mother. There was always conflict between him and his stepfather. He was expected to do a man's work at age 12, and there was no negotiation. He went to Grandma Mary Jane for refuge from George's punishments. I see Uncle John in my infant memories. He was a gentle white haired man who my mother called 'Brother John' Allen. He often stayed with us in our two room log shack along U.S Highway 2 when he was in town from Lodge Pole. He brought my mother bags of groceries and for me, plastic toys that sparkled in their shiny new wrappers. He came and went with his son, Boogie, and his wife, Minerva. Finally, he stopped coming to visit; my mother hardly talked about him without a look of loss on her face. He was buried at the Lodge Pole cemetery in 1955, long forgotten by most, a distant memory for the rest of us.

Uncle Boots, William Allen, Johns younger brother rolled his Bull Durham cigarettes and sipped his FI Muscatel as the legends rolled off of his tobacco stained lips. He told post-traumatic stress stories about the loss of his father when he was just a boy. I listened to his version of the dual between his father, Mr. Allen, and Charlie Perry. "It was four to one, and my dad got three and wounded the other guy, who had a gawt-dam lucky shot as Dad fell to the ground…the dirty sons-a-bitchin' basturds," he lamented. I learned from Uncle Boots many of the fine Lakota skills using the F.I. Muscatel alcohol demon that soothed the family shame. Boots talked about how mean my grandfather George Contway was. "He had a long black bull-whip. If the kids were misbehaving they caught the tail of his whip many times; I wasn't his kid, so I got it twice as bad…I hated him but had to hold my tongue or else," he bemoaned.

Uncle Boots silently rolled another cigarette, then went on with his story, "George was very mean, even to my mother." By this time, George had secretly found and married a second white wife in Dillon. This only served to increase his rough treatment of Julia. If George's steak wasn't cooked just the way he wanted, he would throw it on the floor and make Julia cook him a fresh piece of meat. This went on for several months when one spring morning, she was fed up and had had more than enough of his abuse. Sure enough, George started yelling and threw his steak on the floor again. Without hesitation, Julia purposefully took the cast-iron frying pan from the woodstove, took aim, and gave him a good whack over the head. That was the last time he complained about his steak. He spent more time in Dillon, though; he must have figured white women were less of a threat to his health. George eventually lost interest in the ranch when he learned it wasn't going to be his rightful inheritance. He felt cheated, given years of labor and commitment to the family. After all, he was a philanderin' man and a drifter with a white wife in Dillon.

"Every summer Julia Allen-Hutchin came to visit my mom. She was my mother's oldest Sister, we just called her "Aunt Sis". She took the 374 mile Greyhound bus trip from Dillon to Havre. She usually announced her presence with a two-week advance letter. This usually meant I had to get my bed ready for Aunt Sis and, '…wash out that little bastard Lakota-Chippewa filthy mouth!' My aunt had caught me the summer before talking to Victor, "What a pain in the fucking ass she is when she makes me listen to her boring stories about that gawt-dam son-uv-a-bichen' whiskey still in Ball's gawt-dam Canyon." Aunt Sis for generations told endless stories that nobody else listened to. She was a big raw boned woman like her mother, hardened by her youth and years of selling the genocidal demon alcohol. She was bitter and her lips pursed with old age. It showed in her white privileged arrogance. She told old time stories of riding with her father, William Allen, with a "double tree" buck board team to Dodson, across the mosquito flats to the Phillips County settlement community of the Scandinavian farmers.

Aunt Sis married a white man named Frank Hutchins; he was from Dillon and quite well off. They made their fortune during prohibition bootlegging moonshine to the wards and the non-wards of the government. They sold their 'shine' to most of north-central Montana and in the local honkytonk days in Hill and Blaine Counties. Aunt Sis always bragged that they made the best 'shine' from Valley to Fergus to Hill Counties. She and my mother sat drinking Lipton tea, laughing about the 'revenuers' who came looking for their moonshine still. They never did find it; Uncle Frank had it hidden at the upper end of Ball's Canyon. Aunt Sis and my mother sold the 'shine at local county fairs, pow-wows, and 4th of July celebrations; Thanksgiving, Christmas, and New Years were the main money-making events. As Aunt Sis professed cultural competence, she gave a proficient demonstration of the Mexican cultural tradition they practiced at Servicemen's Bar. Using a Bull Durham cigarette packed with weed, she taught me the multi-cultural Mexican method of our Lakota-Chippewa pegi' tradition. It was a fine skill to be perfected in sacred homage. I have religiously practiced this Lakota-Chippewa tradition for a lifetime.

Frank Hutchins and Aunt Sis later owned Servicemen's Bar in Harlem. Her affluent colorful life following prohibition was afforded through the sale of illegal alcohol to the non- wards over the counter and to the wards out the back door. Aunt Sis was only a 'quarter-breed' Lakota and her white skin allowed her to intermingle in the world of white privilege. She knew my childhood hero, Charles M. Russell, so I listened intently to her stories about him. "Charlie traded his art in exchange for alcohol to drink with the Indians at Lodge Pole. His wife always came to take him back to Great Falls, Montana to paint." It is apparent that Charlie left his seed in Lodge Pole, there are a lot of C. M. look-a-likes on the reservation. Sis's collection of original Russell works dwindled over the years; she sold it piece by piece in her old age to pay for her keep at the Dillon Hotel where she lived. She never had any of her own children She just adopted my half-brother, Chuck.

There were few conversations about my Aunt Grace Allen. On the rare times I did hear my mother mention her, they were fond reminiscences about her deceased half 'Sister Grace'. She died in 1915 from Polio during an epidemic that took many Indian people. There was no treatment for the epidemic, and most doctors showed little empathy for their Indian patients. Grace was several years older than my mother, and her psychic communication with her big sister was ongoing throughout her lifetime. She frequently repeated stories of their late-night discussions. I grew up with the understanding that my deceased Aunt Grace often visited my mom and sat on the edge of her bed. They had specific logical and believable conversations. My mother grieved a lifetime for her big sister. I never fully understood their psychic connection; I always just accepted her accounts as undisputed spiritual Holy Pope Catholic fact.

George and Julia Ball Contway kept up the near 640-acre homestead at Ball's Canyon. Bartholomew and Mary Jane First Holy Woman still spent their summers at the ranch and wintered at 'Lil' Chicago' near the Fort Belknap agency with my grandparents, William and Cecelia Azure Ball. All the Allen kids were still grieving the loss of their father, Colonel William Allen. Yes, the times were a changin', it was the 20th Century. The Indian Wars were a thing of the past, the killing had stopped except for an occasional hanging of an Indian for some suspicious charge, usually for stealing horses or cattle. Horse stealing was still a hangin' offense in Indian country, especially if the thief was an Indian. It was a day of celebration when there was an occasion to hang one of those thievin' dirty bastards; after all, the only good Indian is a dead Indian. The Colburn family still stole government cattle, and the government still let them get away with it. White supremacy ruled the west; the adventurous empire builders hired the guns and bought the bullets.

The Contways worked from sunup to sundown; it was no easy task running a ranch, even with the help of the older Allen children. Aunt Grace was still in good health and was constantly by her mother's side. She was the baby of the Allen children, the family protected her and watched over little baby Grace. My Aunt Nora was the first-born of the Contway children. She was born in 1905 at the homestead place, and she was in a hurry; Contway babies didn't wait for a 3-day buckboard ride to be born in fancy white hospital sheets. She was a true runt and the feistiest of all the Contway litter. Aunt Nora was four years older than my mother. The two went to the Hays Mission School together until they were both taken to Chemawa boarding school in the Oregon Territories. Chemawa was one of the Indian schools that taught Indian children how to be white. They taught them how to appreciate the fine arts, literature and classical music…anything to cleanse them of their own language and culture.

A couple years later Aunt Nora had her first children with Uncle Charlie. I suspect she was feisty and just too dang hard to live with back then, because Uncle Charlie soon fell in love with my Aunt Ella when she was only 16. It was a regular Lakota soap opera elopement drama.

Aunt Nora wasted no time afterward and married Jim Gladeau in 1928 when she was 23 years old. They raised another six kids besides Nora's first three 3/8-breed Lakota-Chippewa landless Indian children. Uncle Jim was one of my very first heroes. He had worked for the Burlington Northern Railroad and was retired; he got 'lots of money' for not working anymore. My uncle pretty much lived for fishing in the summer. He was never without his Lucky Lager beer. I thought he had a pretty good life, all in all. I never did understand why he just liked to drink. I'm sure he had his own Indian story…after all, every Indian story is a sad story. Uncle Jim became a fine role model for the self-determined perfection of Indian alcoholic behaviors. He could get drunk on a Lucky Lager and a mickey of Seagram's 7. He could get so spiritually inclined while singing *The Ol' Rugged Cross* that he would wet his pants, which would be the last straw for my feisty aunt.

Aunt Nora was less than five feet tall and Uncle Jim was over six feet. With her diminutive mighty strength, Nora hoisted him to his unsteady feet. She skillfully guided him from behind, pushing on his Levi-covered butt. She leaned into his backside to get the momentum going. It was obvious this maneuver had been initiated many times before. He had no choice but to move forward like a Burlington Northern freight train powered by my aunt's five-foot stance. She'd point him toward the front door, actually the only door, driving him outside, leaning left to make a roundhouse U-turn. She accelerated her freight train march toward 'The Shack'. The Shack was made of creosote-soaked railroad ties. Uncle Jim specifically built it as his sanctuary on these Lucky Lager and Seagram's 7 occasions. There he slept off the alcoholic dreams that he never seemed to talk about; he just drank more.

By now Ol' Theresa Many Coupes, the midwife, was an expert at delivering Grandma Julia's babies. Her experience came in handy, as my mother was the 'stubborn one' coming into this world in 1909; Julia almost died giving birth this time. My mother, Mayme, was favored by her father, George, but she always looked out for her big sisters and brothers. She was able to calm her father with her softness and natural empathic demeanor. Mayme rarely raised her voice or fussed, doing her best to please her father in spite of his anger toward the other children. She shared her parents with her brother David, sisters Nora and Ella; and her Allen half siblings who were several years older. Julia Contway was 33 years old when my mother was born in 1909. Ball's Canyon was home to the growing Ball-Allen-Contway clan. My mother shared her stories of growing up with her grandparents Bartholomew and First Holy Woman in Lodge Pole during good times as well as bad. They survived the years of abundance and those of drought that scorched the earth from year to year. She enjoyed close and individual relationships with each of her siblings.

The 15-foot long dining table at the ranch was surrounded with wooden benches that always supported a large congregation. The Contway and Allen girls spent their days baking, preparing meals and scrubbing laundry in an old washtub down at the creek. The menfolk and boys worked cattle, tended crops and gathered wood for the winter. There were always fences to mend. My mother and her sisters maintained the gardens and canned the harvest for the upcoming harsh Lodge Pole winters.

It was a time of transition after the turn of the century, time to pull yourself up by the bootstraps. The memories of the Indian genocide and Wounded Knee were fading. The Wernicke–Korsakoff Syndrome confabulations of alcoholic symptoms combined with Lakota memories and distorted drunken dreams. Grace, the youngest Allen sister, was first diagnosed with polio when she was 12 years old. She was bedridden in the hospital for months; the doctors couldn't do anything to save her, and they eventually sent her home to die. My mother, Mayme, took charge of her care until she passed away two years later in 1915.

Terrorist insurgents were at the heart of World War I in 1914 and the news of its devastation was a chilling reminder to our Lakota family. The Lakota still remembered the post-traumatic stress disorders left behind by the great genocide. My grandfather, George Contway, was too old to go fight in World War I by then, but there were a few Lakota, Chippewa, White Clay and Nakoda men who went to fight. The news was heard that it was a massacre of white people, like at Wounded Knee. War was inevitable; tension had been building in Europe since the year of the Blood Moon and the years of the great American genocide. So began The War to End all Wars. Chief Kaiser Wilhelm declared war on the Russian chiefs. There was a Last Stand uprising against those tribal German and Austrian warriors. The first World War began in 1914, five years after my mother was born, and it ended in 1918, the year before my father was born.

The world changed rapidly in the 20th Century. World War I furthered the progressive political success for women's right to vote in 1919. The long fought white women's suffrage movement overcame the white supremacist male dominance that had existed since the revolution. White women took on new roles in manufacturing and made significant contributions to the war effort. Sadly, the struggle for human rights took on little significance for Indian women. Rights didn't mean much, since there were none on the reservations. Abject poverty and starvation continued for Indian people. The Bureau of Indian Affairs allocations of cattle on the hoof were scarce, and all commodities were redirected to the war effort in Europe. At the turn of the century, Indian people were still considered primitive, without measurable worth. They spoke in broken English, but spoke the Lakota language fluently in spite of the beatings they received in school. It wasn't until June 2, 1924, that Indian people were even recognized by the U.S. Government as 'human beings', citizens of our own nation. Homer P. Snyder, a republican from the east coast, sponsored the 14th Amendment to the Constitution, called the Indian Citizenship Act, passed and signed by then President Coolidge.

My uncle usually showed up drunk when he came to see us. My mother made special allowances for Uncle Dempsey; he was a bit 'tetched' after World War II. Named David Contway, Uncle Dempsey was born at Ball's Canyon homestead as the 'Roaring

Twenties' approached and the industrial world exploded. Uncle Boots finally had a little brother to help him with the work and chores on the homestead. Dempsey followed Boots around, like any child follows his big brother. Boots was almost a man by the time Uncle Dempsey was born.

I was told how unmerciful David was to his big sisters; always planning some mischievous shenanigan. Spending most of the summers on his horse hunting and fishing in the Little Rocky Mountains, Uncle Dempsey was quite a cowboy when he was a young man. He had a great Lakota sense of humor and was a 'Coyote' in a humorous way...in a good way. When I was young, he told me the fantastic legend of how he fought the world champion, Tommy Gibbons in a boxing match in Shelby Montana on July 4, 1923. He must have been around 5 or 6 years old then, I would guess.

I listened to his stories about growing up in Lodge Pole, before Pearl Harbor, before the war. He showed me a yellowing photograph he carried in his tarnished wallet of a young man on a horse. He told me about his roan stallion, the one that always bucked him off whenever he heard the whistle at the mine. Dempsey shook uncontrollably trying to roll his Bull Durham cigarettes. Even drinking a cup of hot coffee was difficult; he shook from his war memories of the Pearl Harbor attack in 1942. When Dempsey was drunk, he sometimes reminisced about his teenage years, playing and singing *The Strawberry Roan* with two-fingered guitar chords. It seemed to calm him when he played and sang, but he didn't do it much. David spent his life drenched in alcohol trying to forget the traumatic atrocities he'd witnessed. But still, he was one of my Lakota heroes and a fine contingent mentor in the art of drinking F.I. Muscatel wine. That staple of discerning wine drinking Indians was known as Fighting Indian Muscatel.

The agriculture industry in north-central Montana produced valley sugar beet crops. Immigrant workers from Mexico came for the seasonal production. They hoed beets during the growing season and harvested the beets in the fall. They brought with them the ancestral pegi' medication that was familiar to most indigenous cultures. Aunt Sis and my mother were both familiar with their Mexican traditions from working at the bar. The Rodriquez family did odd jobs for my Uncle Frank Hutchins, gardening, trimming the hedges and tending sapling trees. My mother and her six children lived in Aunt Sis's house after Mom's divorce from Bud Healy. That was in the late 1940's and divorce was the mark of a scarlet letter. Aunt Sis and Uncle Frank had already moved to Dillon, and they left my mother in charge of their property in Harlem. The summer foliage went unattended while she minded the bar, home and hearth.

Mom's brother, my Uncle Pat, was the youngest of the Contway boys. He was born after World War I and was the most adjusted to the white world. He married Rose, a white woman from Malta, who never appreciated the Lakota heritage he shared. I never knew Rose, but she said something to offend my mother around 1937. The comment had something to do with Mom and her 'breed' children. My mother became unusually animated when she talked about her sister-in-law; it seemed like the Hatfield and McCoy family feud. Uncle Pat only stayed for a cup of hot Folger's coffee when he came to visit; his visits were rare and brief. I remember sitting under the table staring at him. He told me I had 'mean eyes'. I don't remember if he ever came back again. My mother told me Uncle Pat secretly came to visit for fear of his wife finding out. Aunt Rose hated my mother, and the feeling was mutual. Uncle Pat worked for the Burlington Northern Railway like Uncle Jim. He too was one of my secret childhood heroes. Pat held an air of importance about him, and I always wondered if he went fishing and drank beer like Uncle Jim.

Chapter 6

12 Gauge Authority

My Uncle Jerry Contway came to visit on random occasions, usually in the summer when all the Indians rode the grub-line and visited their families, telling bullshit stories of great Lakota adventures. His real name was Joseph, but Jerry suited him better and was a name of his own choosing. He was born in 1918 and grew up in Lodge Pole, searching for his escape from reservation life. All of my brothers, uncles and my father always welcomed his humorous stories; they jokingly coaxed him to drink Lucky Lager beer and numbing shots of Seagram's 7. He rarely refused, it was the Indian way. He grew up at Ball's Canyon, though ranch life didn't suit him well. He was meant for city life and bright lights. He was gifted with musical talent and a need to live the life of a musician. My mother reminisced about Uncle Jerry being the embodiment of George, their philandering father, with his charismatic charming smile. He was about 5'8" which was tall for the sawed-off Contway lineage.

Uncle Jerry was a prince charming who played a magic song to the hearts he broke. When World War II broke out, he went willingly, like all of the other men in the family. He fought in the European Theatre, surviving the fear and trauma that millions of men faced in the global destruction. Uncle Jerry never talked about World War II that I remember, he masked the pain with humor. He was never without a smile on his face, with jokes to tell and everyone laughing at his adventurous tales. Uncle Jerry was intent on charming the ladies. They swooned with light in their eyes as he played his hypnotizing Sho-Bud pedal-steel guitar, never taking his eyes off theirs. After the war, Jerry left Lodge Pole forever, although he returned for an occasional brief visit. He stayed a few days at a time, long enough to relive his private memories before starting his long drive home to the Okanogan Valley in Washington state.

The modern technologies of the Roaring Twenties eventually came to Fort Belknap; the government hospital had all of the state of the art equipment. Dentistry and new experimental medications were tested by government physicians on Indian people, like lab rat experiments. My grandfather, William Ball, was almost 50 years old, in the height of his industrious generativist stage. Not only had he learned the family horseshoeing trade from his father, Bartholomew, he also learned the carpentry trade while working at Fort Belknap Agency. He spent long hours building the authoritarian bureaucratic institutional office buildings and driving the U.S. Government nails. My grandmother, Cecelia, managed the home, taking care of their growing number of kids and volunteering where needed. She was 21 years old when she married William in 1899, and for 21 years they made their home in the Milk River Valley of the White Clay at Fort Belknap. They lived in the Fort Belknap 'ghetto' in a three room shack in what we called Little Chicago.

My mom, Mayme, and her baby sister, Ella, shared their childhood stories over Lipton tea and girlish giggles. They grew up together through thick and thin. Ella was born in 1912, and she was three years younger than my mother. They reflected on their childhood sweethearts and beaus and their school days at Chemawa in the Oregon Territories where the intent was to educate them for the white world, removing the ignorance of their primitive reservation existence. Their Indian pot bellies shook when Ella told the story how Aunt Kathryn burned off my mother's hair. She overheated the hot stove poker and tried to use it as a curling iron. They talked about beatings from the Catholic priests and matrons at the mission school. They reminisced about the time their father came to the mission after hearing of these beatings. The priest warned George Contway not to take his children, Nora, Pat, Ella or my mother, Mayme, but he asserted his Smith and Wesson twelve-gauge authority and took his children back to the homestead at Ball's Canyon.

Uncle Charlie was Ella's husband. He grew up in Lodge Pole over the ridge from the Contway place. His first fiddle was made from a cigar box and the neck was carved from an aspen branch. Charlie's sisters were the songbirds of the Laurence-Garvais family. Angela was my mother's best friend for many years. When the family got together, you could swear that the W.S. Walcott Medicine Show was in town. You could hear the gospel singin' and the halleluiahs for blocks away. They got so excited you would swear Jesus was going to come down for a walk on 30 Mile Creek. Charlie told the story of how he learned to play the fiddle. He said 'I just followed the melodies of my sister's voice'. Charlie's first real fiddle cost $2.50 which was a lot of money back in those hard-luck days. Charlie played for dances in Zortman and Landusky, both small mining towns at the south end of the Fort Belknap reservation. He made the long ride to his 'gig', over the Little Rocky Mountains and past Ball's Canyon. He flirted with young Ella as he passed the homestead.

My mom didn't speak directly about it, but it was obvious that Aunt Ella and Nora were rivals. Nora was married to Uncle Charlie first, they had two 'seven-sixteenth' breed kids together. Charlie found occasion to spend time with Ella at family gatherings and community celebrations. I couldn't blame him for his decision; Aunt Nora seemed to be angry at everything and everyone all the time. Ella was such a soft hearted woman; how could she resist his charm? She eloped with Charlie long before I was born. Her musical talents were a match for Charlie's; she played banjo and ragtime piano and had the voice of a songbird. She was self-taught as were all of the musicians in our Lakota family. It would not be long until these two melodious harmonic hearts found each other. It was 'Love in A major' and Charlie and Ella eloped in the middle of the night in September, 1932. My mother was aware of her sister's plans; they were both hopeless romantics. She held her silence and said a quiet prayer for their safety, watching them drive the old Model T into the night.

My grandfather George swore he would kill Charlie if he ever set foot in Lodge Pole again. Charlie was 14 years older than Aunt Ella, and she was the youngest daughter. George was enraged that she did this to him, causing embarrassment to his honor and the family name. It wasn't long before the rumors were rampant; Nora had been abandoned by her husband for her sister. What a scandal it was in the community! George was shamed, Julia held her head high, and my mother secretly kept in touch with her sister. The couple went west to Washington state where they lived while Charlie worked at a lumber mill and Ella prepared for the birth of their first child. Charlie worked on the Grand Coulee Dam and various other WPA and CCC projects in order to make a fresh start and a new lifestyle. Ella learned to drive, finding her own independence away from life at Ball's Canyon and the despair of the reservation.

Over forty years had passed since Bartholomew and First Holy Woman first forged their homestead ranch at Ball's Canyon. George and Julia managed to keep it going, in spite of the looming knowledge that the ranch would never be theirs. It was like a lifetime of anticipatory grief since the authorization and enactment of the Fort Laramie Treaty back in the 1880's. The effects of the genocide were like the insidious creep of the wild morning glory and cheat grass. Bartholomew and Mary Jane took their U.S. Government commodities in exchange for their humility and pride. By the 1920's Wakan Lokahe Win, First Holy Woman, had long ago resigned herself to her identity as Mary Jane Ball. Travel back to the Dakotas was rare, the Lakota nations were still ground zero of the genocide. The extreme poverty was shameless, despair was rampant and there was no shame in their hunger. Mary Jane felt fortunate for the comfort that Bartholomew offered her and her children. They had it better than most for the time being.

It didn't take a whole lot to convince the people living on the reservations that times were tough following the years of genocide by insurgent terrorists. President Calvin Coolidge called for an official government study in 1928, for the status of living conditions in the west following the genocidal atrocities. The Merriam Report became the basis of the Indian Reorganization Act of 1934, which further complicated the government's approach to dealing with the Indian issue. There were still some politicians who swore extermination would have been the most humane. The report revealed poor healthcare, economic devastation, and the failure of the boarding schools to assimilate Indian people into the dominant culture. It indicated deficits in all areas, without fail. Even so, it became the rationale for the Reorganization Act which reinforced the practice of using Indian patients as experimental subjects in covert medical studies, social experimentation of forced relocation off the reservations, and the perpetuation of the 'kill the Indian' boarding school philosophy.

By the time the Roaring Twenties ensued, Bartholomew and Mary Jane were in their mid-70's, he was 75 and she was 74. During the harsh frigid winters, they lived with my grandparents, William and Cecelia Ball, in the Little Chicago suburbs. My great grandfather, Bartholomew, never returned to the home of his white privilege in Pottsville, Pennsylvania, the great American coal country, the ancient earth where dinosaur spirits ascended from the warming coals of our grandfather's fire. He and Mary Jane spent the summers at Ball's Canyon, watching their family grow. Their daughter, Julia, had done well, raising children in a full partnership on the ranch. She could outwork most of the men during hay harvest; she could ride and trail cattle during the fall roundup. Most importantly, she was the protector and matriarch of a huge family. There wasn't much that happened without her knowledge and blessing. George was often gone, and his drinking and anger escalated with his frustration.

In 1924 my mother turned 15 and left Lodge Pole for the Chemawa Boarding School in the Oregon Territories. Chemawa was modeled after the Carlyle Pennsylvania School. Although boarding school was often brutal, my mother also kept fond Oregon memories. She remembered 19-year-old Fred Rinker, a Nez Perce 'half-breed' from the Wallowa Valley. He was an assertive, confident, handsome young man. He showed her how to do the Charleston, and he owned a 1911 Indian motorcycle. They went for long rides on warm summer afternoons, as far as Seaside. My mother worked in the canneries in Salem during the summers as the romance bloomed. When Ella and my mother drank Lipton tea, they dreamily gazed into thin air reliving distant possibilities their futures eventually denied. When their father, George, took sick, Mayme was summoned home. The Great Depression was felt prematurely in the third world of the reservations. I could see from secret smiles and their Lakota eyes the memories of their distant Nez Perce romantic adventures.

The Roaring Twenties was a global phenomenon following the War to End All Wars in 1918; a new capitalism propelled white privilege permanently into socio-economic supremacy. The post genocide for most Indian families created generations of poverty, domestic violence and an insatiable thirsty homage paid to their honorary tribal member. Bud Healy was no exception. His father, Colonel Healy, was a survivor of the genocide. He taught his son well, especially the cycle of domestic violence after a binge with the devil. My mother told me she thought she could change him, but there is no 'unringing' a bell in a divergent personality-disordered mind. Bud had little capacity for empathy, for the hurt and suffering he caused. He and my mother lived at Mud Creek, in isolation from her family. He threatened her, warning he would kill her and the children if she spoke up to her father or brothers. She made excuses for the bruises, the black eyes and broken bones. She wasn't permitted to refuse her White Clay husband's beatings. Her husband had the grace of the U.S. Government and Indian authorities by his tribal rights; she was his property.

Bartholomew lived his life by his bootstraps. He learned to create his empire from the land, depending on nothing but his wit and his partner, Mary Jane. They had their four children and a wealth of grandchildren to show for their years. He lived a life of integrity, protecting and raising his children in a harsh land, a land that took pity on no one. He died of a long life on August 13, 1931, at Lodge Pole. The Creator came to take him home to the white man Jesus, the priest prayed in Catholic Latin. He was buried at their original homestead in Ball's Canyon. Filled with grief and sorrow, First Holy Woman died three months later on November 22, 1931, in the same bed as her husband. After 57 years of struggle and hardship together, Creator took her spirit to the sky with the eagles and hawks giving back her name. She was laid to rest beside Bartholomew on their blood, sweat and tear-stained homestead.

Chapter 7

Geronimo's Cadillac

My father's family was my mother's cousins. It's confusing, I know...you should have been in my head as I travelled a psychic journey of trials and tribulations through this astral transformation. It was a disturbing minefield of psychic expansion. It is a story of this distorted parallel universe I live in. At ten years old this awareness can cause quite a conundrum in a young psyche'. It was a recurring thought I had of my parents and the unspeakable. I had years of unresolved ego function issues as a result. Still, they were my parents; I didn't have any other offers. I loved them anyway and we live with the hand we are dealt. My friend Victor on the other hand, had a typical American story of how he got here. His great aunt and his grandfather came here from Scotland as immigrants. His other grandfather was third generation American, his parents were a reasonable age and most important, his family was blessed with invisible white privilege. No fault of their own mind you, I never held it against him, only jokingly giving him shit, of course.

Years passed, and I still knew very little about my own family on my father's side, yet I knew I felt like an outcast. I was told that Uncle Bob Ball learned Bartholomew's family horseshoeing trade. Bob got rather indignant if you called him anything other than a Lakota Cowboy. The thought of pounding institutional government nails was revolting to his taste, anything to do with 'civilization' was more than enough to get his dander up. He was born decades too late, not to mention in the wrong color skin. He was Gene Autry to the core. Bob was a diminutive man, but he was ten feet tall in his cowboy regalia and big silver spurs. He was born in 1900, the year of the new century. He was 42 when World War II broke out, way too old to volunteer. He worked the U.S. Government cattle for the war effort. The government beef was sent off to war along with his two brothers…Charlie and Johnny.

Uncle Bob, my dad's brother was born to be a 20th Century Lakota Cowboy; he was a champion horseshoer. He left home as a young man, seeking adventure in the old west. He cowboyed around Arizona and the southwest, working from ranch to paycheck before moving on. I guess you could say he was sort of a drifter. He was always looking for the grassy side of the hill. After several years of the wandering life he returned home to the Milk River Valley. Bob finally settled down with Edna Horseman, raising his family in the Little Chicago shack where he was born 50 years before. He worked at the Fort Belknap Tribal Ranch and the Owen Sands Ranch until he 'couldn't hear shit' as my father used to say, and finally retired when he broke his ornery ass. He and Aunt Edna lived in the Little Chicago family home until his ascension to Tex Ritter's "Hillbilly Heaven".

I didn't want to disturb my father's thoughts with my childhood questions and never did know his stories for sure. He rarely talked about his sister, Mary Ann. She was lost in the vast assimilation and accommodation of the repetitive 'oral tradition'.

Mary Ann was born in 1903, and my father spoke fondly when she was mentioned. She was his caretaker when he was a baby; she was his protector from all harm. When he was three years old, he almost drowned in the high water of a spring flood. Mary Ann jumped in the water and pulled him to safety. "All I could see was her hand trying to grab me...she pulled me to shore...saving my life," he said with reverence for his sister. There was never a harsh word in her regard. She was a hard worker, being the oldest girl, with responsibilities for taking care of her younger brothers and sisters. She had dreams for her own life; they were foolish dreams she read about in the dime store white romance novels.

During the Great Depression, Mary Ann met a transient young man who worked at a CCC camp. He was a demolition man; his job was blasting the Snake Butte rock used to build the Fort Peck Dam near Glasgow. He always came to the Saturday night silent movie features at the community hall. His name was Tom Natseway, a hopelessly romantic lad from Winslow, Arizona. Mary Ann was already widowed with a two-year-old child. Three years before she met Tom, her first husband Lloyd Roberts, was killed on the Fort Peck Dam CCC Project. Tom was persistent in his affection, and Mary Ann left with him once the project came to a close. They returned to his home in Arizona, raised a family and found a new life. Mary Ann returned home to Little Chicago only a few times in her life. She returned for her parents' funerals in the late 1930s and once to visit her brothers and sisters. As her health declined, she occasionally wrote to my father. Two of her daughters came to visit once searching for their Lakota roots; that was the last time we heard from her family.

Aunt Josie was a rotund, jolly Lakota-Chippewa woman. She was born to William and Cecelia Ball in 1904 and was my father's second oldest sister. Josie met Ervin Gobet during their years at Chemawa Boarding School in Oregon. He fancied himself as a Salish warrior, doing stunts on his 'war horse'. He did crazy things to impress her on his twice-wrecked, rusted 1903 Indian motorcycle. They chased spring clouds through fields of Lakota-Chippewa Blackfeet-Salish dreams, floating like Crazy Horse visions. They knew each other as friends, their relationship built over time and the commitment was strong.

Aunt Josie married Ervin Gobert, her Blackfeet-Salish "halfbreed", and they lived in the valley of the Catholic mission at St. Ignatius, Montana. The summer I was seven we visited them. It was the only vacation our whole family ever took. One crisp morning we drove to the Moise Bison Range where I'd met Big Medicine, the white buffalo keeper of my dreams. Uncle Ervin and Josie raised a large family of Lakota-Chippewa-Blackfeet Salish children. They lived in the Mission Valley from the time they were married. Ervin worked in logging camps and did construction work for the Bureau of Indian Affairs and the tribal irrigation department.

During the Depression, Ervin worked for the WPA and CCC on local construction projects in order to feed his growing family. It was a struggle; Josie worked at the mission school as a cook and they managed to make a meager but comfortable living for their children. Josie loved her baby brother, Johnny Ball, and she loved me; I could feel it in her hug. Her oldest son, Johnny Cake, resembled my father, and I was drawn to him instantly. I spent most of my time that summer in St. Ignatius with my brother Chic and Johnny Cake, riding around the mountains in Johnny's '38 Chevy Coupe, listening to '50's music on AM radio.

Uncle 'Bart' Ball was an idealistic young Lakota-Chippewa who dreamed his life away. Life on the reservation after the great genocide was in post-traumatic, third-world despair. Bart read books and magazines about a world away…far away from the devastation that covered the reservation like a blanket of fog. He was born in 1910 in Little Chicago in the same shack as his siblings. Bart was mindful in school and excelled in the liberal arts. The idea of menial work was beneath him, cleaning barns and stables was not suitable work for him. He had his eye on Eva Johnson since they were in school. He fell in love; they married and had two daughters. When their marriage fell apart he left Fort Belknap and Little Chicago without telling his family his plans. Nobody knew where he was until a surprise return home, only one time in 1964 to visit his brothers...Uncle Bob, Tommy and my father. He was a rather peculiar sort of man in a very likeable and identifiable way in my pre-adolescent mind.

Bart was quiet, unassuming and unimposing. He treated my mother with polite respect. He didn't get excited and remained private in his thoughts. He and Uncle Tommy had a similar demeanor in that way. They even looked and walked alike. Uncle Bart, the second oldest son didn't drink like all of the Indians at Fort Belknap. Sometimes he disappeared alone, and when he returned he never turned down the offer of food. He lived in anonymity and sanctuary in the hills of Vallejo, California. Bart never returned home again after that one long visit in 1964. The family speculated whether he had come home to say goodbye without disclosing his illness. He was living in Solano County, California, when he left this world in 1978. It was his last stand Indian uprising against the cancer he carried. My Uncle Tommy drove his 1964 Ford pick-up truck to Vallejo to bring his oldest brother back to his long-lost ancestral Lakota-Chippewa-Irish family. His wife, Eva Ball, rests beside him in Lodge Pole in the world beyond this one.

The Indian nations were taken by force; by the 1920's their land was a new American land. President Harding's platform in the 1920 presidential election promised to, "Return America to prosperity…God bless America…God bless this melting pot where all men are free and created equal!" Implicitly he vowed to return America to its white privileged homeostasis. This version of the American Dream was alive with prosperity for Bartholomew Ball's white ancestors in Hershey, Pennsylvania. It was just our Lakota-Chippewa luck. Normalcy for the 'human beings' across the nations was beyond reach. The insurgent terrorists cut our hair, turned our tongues and bought Geronimo a Cadillac. Sitting Bull joined the Wild West Show and the reservation Indians sang their sad songs. To the white man, shame was invisible. To the Indian it was like a buffalo in their path. They relived the post trauma memories of the genocide, without welfare checks and the altruistic graces of the guilty. Every Indian story is a sad story.

Ball's Canyon was returned to the White Clay and Nakoda upon the death of Bartholomew and First Holy Woman, or Mary Jane, as she was known. President Hoover won the 1928 Presidential Election. The country was propelled toward the future, and without warning…the Great Depression and the Wall Street Crash of 1929. The cattle and horses that remained on the Ball family ranch were confiscated by the U.S. Government and sold at auction. The homestead deteriorated into entropic decay.

My mother, Mayme Contway, was stuck in a cycle of violence with Bud Healy. She had four Lakota-White Clay children. The oldest, Timothy, died of the dreaded polio epidemic the year before the ranch auction. My half-breed Kootenai grandfather, George Contway, died on November 5, 1937. He had invested his life into the Ball's Canyon homestead. He was angered and in denial of Bartholomew and First Holy Woman's betrayal and his exploitation to poverty. George's biggest regret was that he had not invested more time and effort in his white family. If only Helen, his bigoted wife, had been an heir to her family's wealth. George's white sons, Arthur and Warren, might have seen their father more often than rare visits when he drifted through Dillon once or twice a year. Rumor had it that he even had a third wife from the Wallowa Valley in Oregon.

The world was becoming 'civilized', survival was dependent on the ability to earn an income, so the Indians cut their warrior hair to learn the white man ways. With it, they left behind their pride in exchange for jobs and their Lakota shame. They looked like civilized Indian politicians, asserting an inherent right to their self-effacing honorary tribal member, boasting their ward of the government arrogance. There were both the elected tribal council men and Bureau of Indian Affairs bureaucrats. They learned to exploit their own people for self-survival, without remorse, without guilt or shame. The white privileged people in Harlem, Montana, bought their big fancy automobiles, electric washing machines and refrigerators. They built houses with water that came right into the house from a faucet, and indoor outhouses with toilets that flushed. They sold wire, copper pipes, lumber and nails to the tribal government and Indians who wanted toilets, too. Opportunist Eddie Cuerth and his Harlem general store made many fortunes from Indian despair.

Uncle Tommy was an Irish-Lakota half-breed, born in 1911 in the Ball family's Little Chicago suburban shack. He was much better suited to the reservation life than my dad would ever be. He often came to visit us with his wife, Alice. My Uncle Tommy was nine years older than my father, and they looked uncannily alike, as did Uncle Bart. Tommy was an older version with graying sideburns and a soft spoken voice. Alice was a Nakoda ward of the government and enrolled at Fort Belknap. They raised eight Lakota, Chippewa and Nakoda offspring. Her maiden name was Pond; my mother talked about Alice's brother, Jimmy Pond. He died from post-traumatic drinking in the early '50s. Alice's son, Babe, was special, he went to live at the mental health hospital in

Warm Springs around the age of 20. He liked to help me put my model airplanes together. He said he liked the smell of the glue.

My cousins Frank and Karen were the next oldest to Babe, both several years older than me. Frank loved to drink beer almost as much as he loved to sing Hank Senior songs in 5/16 time when he'd had one too many. He had a special stool assignment at Kennedy's Bar. When they were younger, Alice's kids Slick, Speed and Monty followed my brother, 'Reverend Jim' on his drinking binges and hunting 'slow elk'. Slow elk are cattle too lazy to run and escape the bullet from an unsteady Seagram's 7 infused hunter. They recovered from their hangovers on soupy hamburger gravy called 'bullets' and frybread. All involved were in various stages of preconscious awareness and remission. My aunt Alice always smiled, she was kind hearted…with kind eyes. She snuck me candy, with a wink and a wave of her kerchief. Her house always had the smell of meat cooking mixed with the smell of baking bread. She and Uncle Tommy lived in the reservation HUD housing in the Self-Help section. These were houses constructed in the '60s, an experimental self-determination program to allow Indians to become homeowners. Ownership was confined to the reservation; this implied bias assured that the reservation Indians would not mix with the backbone of the white middle-class socioeconomic system.

Aunt Kathryn was named by William and Cecelia after our magnificent white privilege aunt, Katie Ball-Sweeney. Aunt Katherine was born in 1913 at Fort Belknap Reservation in the Little Chicago suburb like the rest of the Ball children. By then the small house was overwhelmed with the need to earn more money. They both took on additional work. William took on more jobs at the blacksmith shop and Cecelia scrambled to take in more laundry and sewing. Cecelia had gone to the Flandreau boarding school in the Dakota Territories when she was 13 years old, then to Chemawa where she finished her education.

Aunt Kathryn's tale of burning my mother's hair off with a hot stove poker was much more humorous than my mother's version. Once Katie completed school, she returned to Fort Belknap. It didn't take long before she met Joseph Turcotte. They married and had 8 kids before Joseph had time to learn the Coyote's cruel lesson and died of cirrhosis. Uncle Cecil Bennett quietly stopped drinking and stepped in to raise all eight of Aunt Kathryn's children being a patient, kind loving father. He worked on the Burlington Northern Railroad and was an exceptionally skilled drinker before Joseph's death. He was welcomed into the family overwhelmingly. Aunt Katie and Cecil raised those eight Lakota-Chippewa children.

Uncle Charlie was born in 1916 in the dilapidated White Clay suburbs of Little Chicago. The shanty shack often flooded and filled the family home with white muddy river clay; the flood that year was no exception. The Ball family was at capacity. Cecelia worked day and night in addition to her responsibilities at home. Mary Ann and Josephine were in their teens, parenting their younger brothers and sister. Charlie was curious about physics; he was interested in the theories of a man called Einstein. He read all the journals and scientific literature he could find. When he attempted to fly a kite in a lightning storm, Cecelia caught him trying to electrocute himself in the rain and tanned his backside hide really good. He worked with his father, learnin' the family trades, fantasizing about going to an Ivy-League college back east someday if they ever let Indians study there. It had only been a little over a decade earlier that the U.S. Government determined that Indian people should be considered part of the human race.

After twenty long years of William and Cecelia rearing and raising children, my dad, Johnny, was born on December 20, 1919, in the decay of the Little Chicago shack. He was the youngest Lakota-Chippewa child, the most doted-over of all Cecelia's children. Mary Ann and Josie were more like parents than sisters; they showed special favor to both Charlie and Johnny. My father was called 'Chinkie'. The family story was that he was given the nickname because of his voracious love of rice, but I'm not sure if that was true. It sounded logical so I never questioned his name again. There was a large Chinese population in nearby Havre; even Indians needed someone to look down on once in a while. It made them feel better about themselves. It's only human nature according to Darwinian Theory. Johnny had the mechanical mind of the Ball family. He tinkered with broken down machines from the time he could walk, it seemed. If it was broke he could fix it; if it couldn't be fixed, he would make a better one.

Chapter 8

From Romance to The Dark Cloud of War

My father and Uncle Charlie were inseparable as young boys. They fished and hunted the Milk River in winter and the Little Rockies in summer. They even romanced the Fort Belknap girls together even though Johnny was more interested in the white girls in Harlem. Harlem being the white town across Milk River just off the Ft. Belknap reservation. It was the railhead where the influx of Scandinavian farmers received the goods and plows that were used to rip up our land. Charlie had an easy charm with the White Clay and Nakoda women. His incurable dry sense of humor and hopelessly romantic persuasion impassioned the women he met. He and Johnny talked about their future and a great big world they had yet to explore. Charlie was able to find a bottle of 'hooch' once in a while to spice up the girls, relieving their defenses of feigned prudishness.

Charlie was three years older, the instigator, mentor and big brother. Uncle Charlie was my father's hero growing up. During the Depression they both worked on WPA and CCC work projects to help earn money for the family. Johnny was a teenager, but his mechanical skills earned the respect of his bosses. If it weren't for those government programs, most people would have starved. There were some who felt they were above the back and shovel work, but Charlie and Johnny were only too thankful they could help their parents.

The 20th Century filled with modern technology, the demand for immediate gratification and the ability to take what you wanted. There were warriors like Al Capone and his gang who counted coup on white bankers. There were even rumors that Capone had headed out west. The Ereaux family in Malta, near Fort Belknap, were rumored to have mafia connections. Whether this was true or not, no one was ever certain. Charles Lindberg gave flight like a great silver eagle, soaring across the wild blue Dakota Territory skies. It was hard to imagine, to experience the freedom of the sky and to see the world below. Babe Ruth was the baseball legend who broke the white man record for hitting a ball with a stick. It sounds pretty silly when you put it that way, but…so is the whole game, pointless at best. White people paid him a lot of money while the onlookers cheered and shouted as he ran in circles.

The great dust bowl covered the 'merican Land with a cloud of guilt and shame for the great Indian genocide. To add insult to injury, the U.S. Government built the four presidents' mountain in the Black Hills. Mount Rushmore was a WPA project that created an alcoholic cognitive dissonance across the Lakota land. The monument overlooks the ancestral spirit grounds of the Lakota Nations. It only figured that the white man would search for gold in the Black Hills, breaking yet another treaty. Still, they are in disbelief when they learn that Indians just don't trust them. The invaders really don't believe white supremacy exists; just ask any Indian, their white eyes glow in the dark like devils in the night. They speak like normal people, they walk and act normal, but behind their eyes you can see their feelings. They smile as they take your scarce money in exchange for high priced toxic white man starches, sugar and salt; in exchange for the white man clothing and for breathing white man air. Tourists sometimes hear Itate's whispers in holy Lakota winds.

The tribute to the four white fathers was completed in 1941, near the end of the WPA era. As the next terrorist insurgency was building in Europe, across the nations Indians prepared for the coming Ghost Dance engagement with Nazi Germany, Mussolini and the Japanese Axis of Evil. The beginning of World War II ushered in a new generation of post traumatic Lakota-Chippewa stress disorders. Most of my uncles went to the war and most of them returned. They weren't the same people that left for war; they carried back a hollowness inside them. No man can live in the stench of war and come away without knowing fear and terror…no man, red or white.

Uncle Tommy was often in the doghouse, hiding from Alice at our house. Victor and I sat and listened to the continuing saga of Lakota justice. This time the Lakota were fighting for their captors, fighting for the white eyes' right to oppress them. We listened to my father and Tommy as they told their stories. They sullenly laughed and drank their Lucky Lager beer with nervous caution.

World War II took all of the brothers separate ways. It was rare that they spoke about the War at all with others. The older cousins Buddy Jackson, Boogie and Arnold Allen lived with us at times and their conversations often started out with benign reminiscing about Ball's Canyon, Sittin' Bull and Crazy Horse visions. They joked about the time First Holy Woman got dumped in Milk River filling the water barrels. Johnny purposely spooked the team, the wagon lurched ahead. Grandma Cooshie belly flopped into the river off the end-gate of the wagon. They toasted to Itate' and the four holy winds. The cousins seconded, thirded, and fourthed the toast; they all drank in synchronized Lakota harmony. Uncle Dempsey sat in silence, shaking and smoking his filter-less Camel cigarette, drinking his Lucky Lager beer. My dad and Uncle Tommy relived growing up in the Little Chicago shack along the Milk River and how they listened with great intent to their mother Cecelia's brand new 1934 battery powered Philco radio she rescued from the IHS Hospital. The terrorist insurgency in Europe and Asia was threatening our global peace and the 'merican way of life. In 1941 a dark cloud came over Fort Belknap. The nation filled with worry for impending war with the Nazi insurgence. Bill and Cecelia grew more worried as the dreaded day approached to send three of their sons off to war.

With the growing global unrest, Uncle Dempsey, my mother's brother, was eager to show his Lakota honor and fight for his country. He was 25 years old when he joined the U.S. Army in 1941. His assignment was at Pearl Harbor. He was thrown from his bed the infamous Sunday morning when the Japanese Zeros struck. He trembled and his voice quivered as he told his stories. After the war he was shell shocked, battle fatigued, in post-traumatic stress disordered terror living with his memories of surviving the attack. He was never the same when he came back from the war. He took another drink as he recounted his story to me and Victor when we were little, "I was shaken from my barracks as the first bombs struck. I remember crawling to the window to see what was happening. There were Jap planes everywhere. I could almost see their smiles as they flew by, they were that close. Bombs were going off all around…everywhere. My bunkmate was blown in half right in front of my eyes." Inescapable memories leaving him helpless and shaken to the core, he took another drink as the tears flowed from the corners of his eyes.

By the time the U.S. Government intervened in in 1942, Dad's oldest brother, Uncle Bob, was 42 and too bow-legged to fight for his country. The family all knew Bob well and kindly chuckled at my Uncle 'Cowboy Bob'. "Didn't he work government cattle out at the Sand's ranch?" Jay asked. "No…I think he worked for the tribal ranch…I remember I was a little kid and I used to go help him," Boogie interjected. Boogie was the older of the two brothers and Buddy was the oldest of all three. "He worked for both places I'm pretty sure." Tommy agreed with him, "I used to get letters from mom and she told me all the happenin's back home." "You could be right, you know. I should go see the ol' coot one of these days. Edna is probably tired of his grouchy ol' hide by now," my father chuckled. Uncle Cowboy Bob and my father were never close as there was a 20-year difference in age between them.

My Uncle Bart was 32 years old when the war started. "Didn't he already start a family with Eva…Johnson …or was it Roberts?" Boogie asked, taking a sip of his Lucky Lager. Tommy and my dad shook their heads. "He never did get over that, did he?" Tommy said with my father nodding in agreement, "Probably why he left." Bart was the original 'conscientious objector' and had internalized all the stories he had heard from First Holy Woman about the genocide. The men folk all drank in unison as the oral history continued. Uncle Bart wanted no part of death and destruction, or the responsibility for others living and dying. The world is a savage place; there are choices you have to make if you are going to survive. Uncle Bart withdrew from the world, withdrew from the reservation, in search of self-determination…finding his own path with or without Eva.

Uncle Tommy told his tales of adventures in the African desert where the 2nd Calvary Division built airstrips for a U.S. Army offensive. He was 31 when he and his brothers, Charlie and Johnny, separated at Fort Missoula, Montana. He was sent to Fort

Lewis in Washington state, then reassigned from Fort Benning to a U.S. Army division in North Africa. The campaign was already two years in progress when American forces arrived. The British had held colonial interests in Africa since the 19th Century. The capture of oil depots, destruction of oil wells and disabling of Germantransportation corridors was the 2nd Calvary's task at hand. Uncle Tommy went on about *Operation Torch*, "We met little resistance. By then the Nazis had taken a beating; the outcome was only a matter of time. The Tunisian Campaign followed... sending Hitler and Mussolini...sending the Axis in retreat." The Nazi Panzer divisions were diminished, tanks lying helpless in the African desert. The infamous 'Desert Fox' (Field Marshall Rommel) and General Von Arnim retreated in failure from the African theatre.

"Take care of yourself little brother," Charlie smiled at Johnny. "We have a lot of life yet to live when we get home." Johnny was scared and shaking as they parted, wondering how he would survive without his big brother to watch out for him. Terrified, he was sure he was going to die in that strange jungle. "I'll be okay, Charlie, just be sure you get home safe...you know how mom worries all the time," Johnny replied. Uncle Charlie was 26 years old when he and my father parted in Guam. Little did he know it was the last; the parting goodbyes were brief. They gave one last glance, departing for their separate air transports to their jungle destinations. They shared childhood; they shared their whole life together. "I gotta go...my company is waiting," were Charlie's last words as he boarded the B-52 transport to take him to his final assignment. The 'War to End All Wars' failed its title, and this time the Japanese had attacked our Lakota brothers at Pearl Harbor in Hawaii. The U.S. Government sent Lakota-Chippewas to fight this war. Many of the White Clay People, Nakoda, Navaho Code Talkers, and even the Irish went to fight this war.

My father, Johnny, was 23 years old when he joined the 163rd U.S. Infantry. He and Charlie were both assigned to duty in the Philippines. MacArthur had evacuated the Philippines when it fell to Japan in 1942. By 1944 the Allies had regained strength in Mindanao using long range bombers. Shortly thereafter, MacArthur overran Marotai in the Dutch Indies and Guam. Japan was obviously losing the war, but showed no signs of capitulation or surrender. My father learned of his brother's death while clearing a jungle-covered airfield in his faraway memory. Uncle Charlie never returned to the valley of the White Clay or his 'Little Chicago' home. He was the first Native American to earn the Medal of Valor, but there were no parades or fanfare - just another dead Indian to be missed by his weeping mother. For 21 years I heard my father's screams of silent pain; like 'Big Medicine' the thundering silence infused with the meta-soul forever. I helplessly tried to scream out to him, but he didn't hear me.

I could see the post-traumatic grief and guilt that sat in his steely blue Lakota eyes. The guilt of living, that he didn't lose his life in the Philippine jungle instead of Charlie. When he drank with his 'brothers in arms', they filled him full of bullshit stories that his brother Charlie survived and had been seen in passing. The rumor was that he lost both of his legs in a firefight with the enemy and didn't want his parents to see him in such a helpless condition. My father murmured his World War II nightmares and terror in his sleep. He fought the enemy in his dreams. He spent 32 years drinking away his night terrors. As with many of his comrades, he left his U.S. Army memories in a regiment of Seagram's 7 bottles.

Uncle Jerry, Mom's younger brother, didn't show any overt signs, but it was apparent he slept with his own war horrors. When World War II came, he went. He managed to survive the experience, in body anyway. As most survivors, he entertained a life of alcoholism to forget his own unspoken horrific post-traumatic dreams. Uncle Jerry lived life on the fragile edge, on the edge of disaster. After all, he was a musician. When he came home he was on the run from his demons. They always followed him, drawing him back; there was no escaping them. His laughter covered the fear, his smile disguised the terror. His drinking 'to forget' destroyed his relationships, leaving his children without their father. Even though he knew better, he couldn't stop the demons from chasing him. There were times when he was weary, wanting to find something normal, but circumstance never let him find peace.

Chapter 9

No Dogs, Indians or Lakotas Allowed

Julia, my 'half-breed' Lakota grandmother was slowing down with age. She lived out her life in Lodge Pole where she was born. She was 88; it had been 14 years since my grandfather George Contway passed. Julia was the matriarch of the family, and my mother Mayme took care of her during her long illness. Finally, she was laid to rest in 1951 at Lodge Pole Cemetery. She was from the last generation of the Indian Wars and the genocidal traumas. Grandma lived with the destruction left behind, a legacy for every Lakota family to pass along in their ancestral stories. Our birth-right was generations of post-traumatic idiopathic stress and the assimilation and accommodation of our descending relevance in the web of life. The Indian on the street had less value than any black man. They were considered less than dogs, assumed twice as ignorant as any white man and their scalps worth more dead than alive. After all, Indian scalps, buffalo hides and Native American artifacts were in big demand in Europe.

The dysthymic idiopathology of a Lakota-Chippewa childhood in Harlem, Montana…the etiology of abject poverty…worse yet being born Indian…even worse a half-breed who doesn't belong in a white or Indian world…here or anywhere. I was born a Hunkpapa-Oglala-Sissiton- Whapeton-Chippewa-Cree-Kootenai-English-French-Mexican Irish Mick as I was told long ago. I sometimes wonder if my memories are projections from my psychedelic kaleidoscopic mind or if they are the actual oral traditions of my mother and father. Perhaps they are Crazy Horse memories of the world behind this world or a psychic resolution of developmental ego-integrity versus despair. Like our Lakota ancestors, I was forced to face a bureaucratic Ghost Dance in the white world. It was a matter of survival through a meta-physical journey of trial and tribulation. It was an astral transformation, a minefield of psychic expansion and erosion in these fleeting times, a story of marginalization in this distorted parallel universe. After all, every Indian story is a sad story.

There was a lot of information for my adolescent mind to absorb. The stories I heard over and over from all my relatives, in sometimes slightly divergent accounts of romanticized fact. I learned Catholic guilt from both of my parents. You know the stories, "…We walked up-hill both ways" …the stories about the Great Depression, the tough times suffered. My mother and father were from the generation that learned to survive on the scorched prairie earth of the Fort Belknap reservation. Life was extreme poverty and despair. It was a time when Indian hearts filled the Milk River with their tributaries of tears. The genocidal sin of the Great White Fathers left its eternal scar on the red road of Indian dreams. All the rich people found their grief in the capitalistic stock exchange. Poor white people suffered in poverty and learned the Lakota-Chippewa way. They jumped from windows to their deaths because they lost their wealth. When things got better, it only got better for white people. There was no recovery in the reservation 'stock exchange', no recovery was intended.

My mother Mayme managed to keep her smile in spite of it all. Harlem, Montana, was not kind to Indians in general, especially single Indian women who were targets for gossip and rumor. It was a conservative community. The white bureaucrat social workers came around once a month, sporting their briefcases. They wielded useless rhetoric. They espoused bio-psycho-social horseshit, threatening to put us kids in foster care away from our home. I felt responsible for our poverty even though I had no control over our social despair. My father was rarely around; he preferred isolation and solitude. Harlem's Main Street was four blocks long. U.S. Highway 2 ran east-west for a mile through the town, parallel to the Burlington-Northern Railroad tracks and past our two room log shack. The post office was there, and community leaders had well established businesses on Main Street. The white people of Harlem were mostly high school educated; most Indians never made it that far. The expectation for an Indian was to be a good Tonto.

Harlem is just off the reservation, but its population was mostly white and there was no question that they were in control. The thought of an Indian owning anything was absurd and held a certain implausibility. Indian people weren't allowed to be anything other than somebody else's 'prairie-nigger'. The Jim Crow south was alive and well in Harlem; the enforcers just didn't wear hoods. After the genocide, the hatred wasn't always spoken, but Indian kids felt the implicit bias on a daily basis from the white kids at school, from the teachers and school administrators. We had already learned to feel the shame of poverty. They found many ways of telling us Indian kids we were stupid and would never amount to anything. We took them at their word...with great intent we did our best to fulfill their prophecy. Fortunately, Victor was afforded the luxury of white privilege. It didn't hurt that his grandfather was the county sheriff, and his other grandfather an important business leader in the community. Even though Victor was poor, he did have some advantages. He never bragged about it in the way the Parks family did, with their ostentatious vacations flaunting white supremacy.

Victor and I often shared our experiences. His life was pretty normal, an American way of life. He knew all four of his grandparents, they were well respected in the community. Even his aunts and uncles were well respected. He had a few that drank too much, but everybody drank too much in Harlem. His Uncle Blaine, Uncle Bill and Aunt Betty drank respectfully and Jay and Alice drank with the Northside Spirit. Me on the other hand – I was born into a huge confused and chaotic family of post-traumatic alcoholism. We lived in a two room log shack along U.S. Highway 2 which was about 20 feet out the front door with dusty bare hardpan dirt for a front yard. About 75 feet behind the shack was the Burlington-Northern Railway. Harlem, Montana, the kind of town where everybody needs someone to look down on, someone to make them feel better about themselves.

Victor's mom and dad were both young, in their early twenties when he was born. They lived in Ketchikan, Alaska, when Vic was a baby. His dad worked in the lumber mills, and they lived in a lumber camp. Victor had his mother and his dog Princie there to protect him. It was years before his sisters were born. He was the oldest and had three blond younger sisters. It was a picture of the American dream except for the drinking. My mother, on the other hand, was a divorced Lakota woman with God knows how many Lakota-Chippewa-White Clay half-breed children. She was 45 years old when I was born. She was not one of the worthy poor white women, but the Welfare Department had no choice but to help her as she was a 'non-ward' of the government. The U.S. Government considered her legally white. We were not enrolled, 'pedigreed', bona-fide, U.S. Government-approved Indians. What a dilemma – I was a 'three-eighths breed' Lakota-Chippewa according to my State of Montana birth certificate and her young lover Johnny's only son.

Mayme drank Lipton tea and reminisced with her sister Nora. Although my mother thought she could change Bud Healy, there were a lot of broken promises. Her intention was to save him from himself, as most women try to do when they are in love with anti-social narcissists. He showed her how much he cared for her with random beatings, threats and intimidation. He kept her pregnant; four of my six half-siblings were born before World War II. My mother was not a very good Indian woman; she had the courage to leave him. In the 1940's the best thing for a 'good' Lakota woman was to take her Gros Ventre husband's beatings, physically and emotionally. She finally divorced him in 1950 when the alcoholic judge saw with his own eyes the evidence of alcoholic beatings and domestic violence. She showed the judge her black eye and the bruises on her arms and back where he kicked her.

After my brother Marvin finally retired from the U.S. Army in the '70s, he lived at the south end of the Low Rent ghetto at Fort Belknap with his father, Bud Healy. During my adolescence I repeatedly heard my mother's stories of Bud Healy's unmerciful beatings. I always imagined an imposing huge man. Once when he was recovering at my brother's from one of his alcoholic binges, I met the pitiful man. Decadent in years, his time in the bottle had taken its toll. He was wheelchair bound, remarkably scruffy and smelled of respired alcohol…a stereotypical Indian tradition, unfortunately. I began to realize the loss of ego function as I watched this trans-generational dysfunction manifest before my eyes. This was a staggering glimpse of the 'cyclical' nature of alcohol, family violence and the long trauma history my mother and family endured the years before my world began.

My mother was much older than her 45 years when I was born, lost in her Lakota poverty. She really hadn't intended to give me her life filled with racial prejudice, discrimination and poverty. She had already lived many hard years of domestic abuse and White Clay beatings before I came into her world. She was never sure of her age. The government had no reason to maintain records of Lakota *shadow people.* She searched her entire life to find her U.S. Government 'pedigree'. She was told her birth records were lost in the fire of 1934 at Fort Belknap Agency. Apparently, the records of many Indian people were lost in that fire. Without a birth certificate, she was not a human. The audacity of the government... telling this woman that she was not a human. Mayme lived more humanity than all of the bureaucrats in Washington D.C. Her ancestors were imbedded in this land, hunting buffalo and growing crops for food, living in community systems and the rule of tribal law. It was now a land of white laws for white men.

I was an illegitimate bastard Lakota-Chippewa child of incestuous parentage. It was no secret in Harlem, as much as I hoped it was. I often felt the vibration of hushed tones in savage color, saw the finger pointing out of the corner of my eye. The shame and guilt I felt went along with being an Indian from the north side of the tracks. That's where Harlem's poorest people lived, both Indian and white. I was born nine years after World War II ended. My father found his Lakota-Chippewa post-traumatic grief in the Philippines. His thoughts were with Uncle Charlie, rest his weary soul. I never knew Charlie, I didn't really know the ones who did come back: Dempsey, Jerry, Tommy or my dad...but, I always seemed to find myself to blame for his sadness. My mother affectionately called my father 'Johnny'. She told me that's what Gramma Cecelia called him when he was little. Her sons Charlie and Johnny were always full of mischief, "like two peas in a pod," she would say, then sigh and shake her head.

In the world of structural mechanical organization and applied engineering, Johnny was a remarkable man; his skill fascinated me despite being well beyond my comprehension. Perhaps it was an inherent genetic predisposition, a mutation of horseshoeing of sorts. He was a skilled carpenter and craftsman. Most Indians aren't expected to excel beyond the blue collar trades. I am guessing he learned valuable skills in the U.S. Army during World War II. It was his aptitude, tinkering with anything mechanical. I tried, but couldn't appreciate grease the way he did. I took things apart very well, but it was putting them back together that was the challenge. He gave me a pathetic look of failure – his failure, and I was a reminder. None-the-less, he was my dad, although it didn't say so on my birth-certificate. I just took my mother at her word. You couldn't tell it by our natural abilities. He was still my hero and a great Lakota, a large, hook-nose stereotype with steely blue eyes and dark skin. He was barrel chested like Sitting Bull and equally as wise.

I was born in the astrological spring, the new beginning of the Aries constellation. I eventually learned that all things of the universe are part of the 'web of life', even though I scoffed with Anglo rejection. The encounter with the great buffalo, Big Medicine, when I was four recurred to remind me...*Look down on no one, look up at no one.* I would see a lifetime of challenges as hopeless as a Crazy Horse vision. My father's memories were reminders of our unresolved relationship. We grew closer in our prolific silent psychic dysfunction. I made my first effort when I was nine or ten months old to talk to him. Johnny grinned at me, picked me up and placed me in the middle of the patchwork quilt bedspread. He told me mindless stories of how he used to love candy when he was a kid. He methodically took the shiny paper off, to find the chocolate treasure wrapped inside. He talked about his 'Aunt Katie' who married the man who made sweet tasting Hershey's chocolate as I felt it melt in my mouth. He never seemed to be interested in what I had to say.

My brother Chic was my protector, and I always looked to him to come to my childhood rescue. He was 12 years older than me; he was a bit mischievous and wore a perpetual shit- eating grin. You could never anticipate his next prank. Chic's job was to haul water in a five-gallon milk can in his Red Flyer wagon. We made the three block journey to Laura Malley's house. She was a poor widowed white woman who befriended my mother. Perhaps it was because they were both poor with a string of kids, or my mother was always polite enough to listen to Laura's endless chitter-chatter about nothing in particular. It took at least half an hour just to say 'good morning' at the Malley house. Laura's husband died a few years before, and she was left to raise their five children alone. Every day Chic pulled the Red Flyer around to the front door of the log shack. He helped me with my coat and rolled the big milk can out the door. I struggled to get the can in the wagon, while he laughed at my effort.

My job was to help him by sitting on top of the milk can to 'hold' it in the wagon. He convinced me it was the most important job as we bumped and rolled down the dusty gravel highway toward home. It was his way to make me feel important and keep me from an unintentional head-on challenge with the high speed traffic on U.S. Highway 2. He was in Boy Scouts and lived by the code of honor. He was quick to help an elderly person carry their groceries or help them cross the street. Often he came running in the log shack to get food and water for the hobos passing by in the Burlington Northern freight cars. Chic was more likely to find work than most, his optimism a plus. The bright side was always within reach as far as he went. His best friend, Bobby Shafer, spent most of his time at our house. The two of them hunted pheasants, rabbits and deer to help feed our family. There was no refrigeration, just an apple box framed in the window so the contents could take in the cool of the night. It worked as well as a refrigerator in the winter freeze. Most of their free time, the two of them tinkered with Bobby's '38 Chevy Coupe. It was held together with baling wire, rusty nuts and bolts.

I was aware of the many children in our family by the many legs and feet. Some of them were actually 'half breed' half-brothers and sisters. Some were orphaned throwaways, rejected by their parents and by themselves. It was a disappointment to know they had given up on themselves. My mother always took in the waifs and castaways. This was my preparation for my 21st Century Quest; fated by my Lakota heritage and genetic link to my mother's Lakota empathy and implicit compassion. There was always room for one more body seeking shelter on a freezing Montana night. The extra bodies were either related or friends of my brothers or sisters. My cousin Marlene stayed with us often. She was Uncle Bob's step-daughter. Jimmy Legge was the most regular; he was orphaned at seven years old. His brothers raised him, when he wasn't staying at our house.

Again I desperately tried to talk to my father, but he couldn't hear me. It was in 1955; we lived in the two room log shack at the east end of Harlem. It was on U.S. Highway 2, as you go out of town. I watched him fill the old blackened pot with water from the milk can near the door. He put the eggs in the steaming water as it heated. He stirred the wood stove, threw in a chunk of wood to increase the burn. He turned and took a puff off of his Bull Durham cigarette. He mindlessly talked about how his mother taught him to boil eggs when he was young and he would teach me when I was old enough. I never did get his attention, and he never did notice I was trying to talk to him. Our silence increased year by year, never knowing what to say to each other. We soon moved to a five room mansion on the north side of Harlem that my mother rented from Sarah Miller. Life was never the same; change is forever. Harlem's north side stretched from the railroad tracks to the bridge at 30 Mile Creek. The north-north side is north of the bridge, where the poorest of the poor lived in Harlem. You see, even as children there was socio-economic class distinction. You didn't notice it if you were white, but if you were one of the poor prairie-niggers, it slammed you in the face every time you turned around. The mansion was several dilapidated shacks nailed together. The worn roof leaked in synchronicity when it rained. The sound of the rain dripping in buckets made harmonious rhythms. My mother strategically placed pots and pans around the room to catch the rainwater. There were holes in the walls from the previous tenants and a tired, worn linoleum floor. The upright gas heater in the 'front room' worked overtime during the cold 40 below zero winter nights.

The most coveted feature of the house was the running water, not like running water as you might imagine with a kitchen sink and toilet that flushes. Out of the floor in the main room was a galvanized pipe with a shiny copper faucet at the end. My mother purposely placed her 30-gallon washtub to catch any dripping water for reuse washing clothes in the newly acquired wringer-washer machine. My nephew Jerry and I played while my mother, my sister Annette and my sister-in-law Joan worked on washing a massive pile of laundry. Jerry touched the roller on one side to feel the smooth turning of the machine. I, on the other hand, stuck my fingers in the side that sucks the clothing in and wrings the water from the fabric. I attempted to pull away, but the machine had me, dragging my three-year-old arm into the unyielding grip of the rollers. Jerry panicked and ran, knowing he would be blamed for the incident. Joan was the fastest; hearing me scream, she came running to free me from the unrelenting pull of the machine.

My sister Annette was 16 years older than me. Her son Jerry is 17 days older than me. There was usually a group of kids around; we all argued and fought as toddlers and adolescent peers and rivals. Jerry pushed Johnny Ray Adams, Bitsy Bear's son, into the upright heater, forever branding his ass with little square imprints of the heater grate. Terry Cole, Tiny Bear's son, was always around. He and Jerry usually ended up fighting over some useless challenge of superiority. They were both alike, making choices without thinking. Sister Annette and the Bear girls were friends. Annette was drawn to the bad boys; she took up with Buzzy Bear and left home. He was in and out of prison, and my sister glorified the life of crime. She forced Jerry and his younger sister Doll into the life…she beat it into them. Annette was violent and mean when she drank. My mother did her best to get Annette's babies away from her, but the welfare department did nothing, they were just Indian kids. They were left to raise themselves. Jerry and Doll would go to the mission for food, until my sister caught them and beat them for being hungry.

There was a shorter height faucet in the tiny kitchen of the five room mansion. It was next to the antique gas stove that needed to be manually lit with a match every time it was turned on. Beneath the faucet was the 'slop pail' for kitchen waste and night time urination and defecation when it was cold. My mother obsessively emptied and cleaned that nasty slop pail twice a day, sometimes three when I had a nasty outbreak of the 'Rocky Mountain highsteps'. I thought nothing of it as many of the White Clay and our Nakoda relatives also had slop pails, but they were too poor to have running water. Most of them didn't even have electricity. Life was much like it was after the genocide, the infestation of poverty and its dangers. With destitute poverty came despair, commodities, alcohol and eating disorders – the wonderful bread my mother baked with the USDA commodity flour, the gravy, those wonderful starches, even the frybread's insidious diabetic creep.

The five room mansion was surrounded by weeds that grew and died with the seasons. The summer months provided cover for many Indian Wars, fighting at John Wayne's side, as well as childish experimentation with my well experienced cousins. Past the leaning clothes line and the garbage barrel, down the path through the weeds was the wooden 'outhouse'. There was a wooden seat and a stack of the yearly Sears and Roebuck catalogues. There was also a fallen down shack, probably a chicken coup at one time, past the outhouse and surrounded by a huge field of weeds. There was an open pit 'slop-hole' where we emptied countless buckets of 'slop', the daily mixture of urine and feces, along with egg shells and bacon grease from the kitchen. There was a Diamond Willow wind barrier following the irrigation ditch sheltering the view to the Swendside's property line. Other than our poor family, nobody but Victor and Billy Ragsdale were allowed into my private playground. The Ragsdale Ranch was much like our rundown house but it included a barn of the same quality. We had already learned to feel of shame of poverty.

Thanksgiving is a day for white people. Indians have nothing to give thanks for; it's a reminder of what we've lost. We graciously eat turkey, just because it's a reason to feast. That year our feast was deer meat that Chic poached, a pot of pinto beans and homemade bread. Pretty much just another day. We were out of school and that was a blessing. I went to get Victor late in the afternoon. My mother figured his family was done with their Thanksgiving celebration. There were several cars there; you could hear their laughter and guffaws as you entered the wooden porch to Victor's house named 'Big Pink'. Pete and Edna Seimens were there, and Chub and Gloria were visiting from Ennis. Chub worked for the railroad; Gloria was Alice Miller's younger sister and Victor's aunt. They were gambling with real money, piles of change, ones, fives, tens and even a few twenties in the pot. They were drinking Lord

Calvert whiskey and Budweiser beer. That was my first sight of Thanksgiving in the white world.

A few weeks later, my mother cooked for days making pies, cakes and loaves of homemade bread. My father showed up in unusually good spirit and boastfully made his mother's recipe of chocolate fudge and cookies with all colors of sweet stuff on top. My mother clipped the small branches from the tree my father brought home, putting them on top of the antique upright gas heater. The tree was propped in the chilled, frosted corner of the room, and its sweet aroma filled the air. It was a freezing cold evening with sub-zero temperatures. The water faucet was left dripping to keep it from freezing; water filled the ice cold tub strategically placed under the dripping faucet. My mother randomly took pots of water into the freezing cold night so the tub wouldn't overflow. She emptied them by the rusty old trash barrel. We took turns going into the dark night. It was one of my few good Christmas memories.

I guess it was no secret; everyone in town knew we was poor. Pete Goodheart came by in a Santa suit to drop off a food basket from Merry Market. My mom was unable to appreciate the basket, she was worried sick – her grandchildren, Jerry and Doll, were alone with nobody to take care of them. She worried in frustration and went to the welfare department, "Annette uses them for a meal ticket…that's all she wants them for. Her idea of a celebration is drinking up her welfare money in the Helena bars."

Compared to Jerry and Doll, I had a relatively stable life. At least my mother didn't drink, and she was always home. Annette was overt in her dysfunction. My brother Marvin often called Babe, on the other hand, tried to disguise his alcoholism behind his covert U.S. Army uniform. He attended military social functions to give administrative status to his dysfunction.

Chapter 10

The Fine Art of Assimilation and Accommodation

Most Indian people are migratory by nature, following the seasons. The genocide disrupted these patterns. They long for the pow-wow highway. It is an unexplained phenomenon, a yearly event as winter turns to spring. We didn't have a car so we couldn't join in the traveling. My mother's house was a designated stop because we were always home.

There were relatives from everywhere who came to visit. Sometimes they stayed for a few days, some stayed for a week or two. There was no designated time to come or leave. We were on Indian Time, it determined when you got here and when Creator moved you to push on. My mom never turned anyone away, always cooking and a hot pot of coffee always on the upright heater. This kept the house lively, listening to the Lucky Lager adventures and drinking Folgers coffee. The weeks of spring were filled with visitors coming and going down the gravel pow-wow highway.

When the Trouchies came to visit, it was usually for several days, maybe even a week. They were my grandmother's French Canadian relatives, scattered about in Alberta and Saskatchewan. It was a huge and growing family. They were a part of the Azure clan, the family extended to the Dakotas and most of Montana. The Trouchies visited their way across the land as there was a lot of family between Wolf Point and Great Falls. Harlem was their first stop coming south across the border to the United States. When they weren't off socializing with the Azure family, my mother and the Trouchie women visited and drank countless cups of Lipton tea. When they weren't drinking tea, they were cooking. My father and the men sat around drinking Lucky Lager beer, joking about Sitting Bull and their own Lakota-Chippewa adventures, laughing off their shame.

I first met my grandmother, Cecelia Azure Ball, when I was only a year old. She came to our house with the Trouchies. They were on their way to Lewistown for the Metis Celebration. My dad's nephew, Frank, was going to play in the 'old time fiddlers' contest'. He practiced up all year and couldn't miss this chance. His brothers joked about his out of tune ear, challenging his determination. My grandmother Cecelia doted over me. I was her youngest Johnny's only son, which was all that mattered. She was a generous, kind Chippewa woman, always laughing and teasing. She smothered me with grandmother hugs, squeezing like she was never going to see me again. She also paid attention to Jerry and Doll. They were left with my mother in the middle of the night and had been with us for quite a few weeks. Jerry and I were playing with matches, trying to light dust bunnies. My sister Barbara tried to scold us, so I whacked her with my toy ball peen hammer. My grandmother muttered in her Chippewa language, vigorously waved her cane in the air, and saved me from the wrath of my sister. I hid behind her skirts until Barbara went away in frustration.

Like the passing season, my mom's sister Ella and her husband Charlie showed up like clockwork. They came to see Uncle Charlie's family, and it was always time for celebration. Aunt Ella and my mother were like schoolgirls, happy to see each other. It was a long way to the Okanogan Valley, so we only heard their stories of how much better life was in Washington. Their visits were always a happy time filled with music.

Charlie was a fiddle player, his fiddle was attached to his hip and he was always ready to play a tune. The families that lived at Fort Belknap were always ready with their guitars for a ho-down. Ella beamed at Charlie as he sawed out the notes to the Tennessee Waltz on his weathered fiddle. All the Lakota-White Clay-Nakoda-Chippewa-Kootenai musicians came out of the woodwork when the feast and frybread flinging started. The music and stories sometimes lasted for days. The nights of drinking Lucky Lager and Seagram's 7 grew shorter with the years, then one year it stopped altogether.

The spring of 1958 was a quick thaw; the muddy water was up to the door. We were forced to leave our five room mansion. Jim Harvey, the taxi driver, gave us a ride to Wagner. We stayed for two weeks with Aunt Nora and Uncle Jim waiting for the flood water to recede and dry up enough for us to return home. Wagner was 10 miles west of Malta on U.S. Highway 2. Nora and Jim lived in a small two-bedroom wood frame house with all their kids. Carol Dean was their youngest, she and my sister Barbara were the same age. We visited several times during the summer. It usually involved a family feast, music, dancing and of course more alcohol. When we visited, the evening usually ended with everybody at the Wagner Bar with my Uncle Jim and Dempsey. My mother and Aunt Nora sat in her living room, drinking tea and endlessly worrying. That is what Lakota women are born to do. By the end of the night, the party moved to the shack behind the house. Carol and Barbara sang and played their guitars into the night. There was always plenty of Lucky Lager beer and a few bottles of Seagram's 7 to pass freely.

On the random occasion that one of my older brothers was home on leave from the army, we loaded up in the old dilapidated '48 Chevy Coupe that one of them bought for $25 from Dolven's Chevy Garage. The doors were held closed with baling wire; it smelled of anger, dust, alcohol, perfume and the faint odor of sex. We always visited Uncle Raymond Helgeson and Aunt Dora. It was on our way to the old homestead at Ball's Canyon. Dora was the daughter of Chief Nosey. My mother spent a lot of time with Dora becoming close friends when they were kids going to the mission school. We stayed at the Helgeson's, a fitting Indian name for the better half of the day.

Dora, Raymond and my parents reminisced about the Depression and the days of the Zortman mine. The land was part of the Fort Belknap Reservation until gold was discovered. The U.S. Government gave the tribes worthless land on the east end of the reservation in exchange for this gold-laden land. White miners laughed and joked at how those Metis fiddle playing French Cajun Indians assimilated like horses after the Indian Wars. They copulated fiercely with the White Clay and Nakoda women, those no good half breeds.

Lamebull, Chief of the White Clay, was always at odds with the Nakoda Assiniboines. They couldn't agree on much, which forever kept the tribes in conflict. The government agents were quick to agree with both sides, keeping them arguing over conflicted tribal policies. The government pretty much had the final say regardless of the tribal outcomes. The same dynamics were played out in our family relationships. Sooner or later the much debated Perry-Allen murder came up. Charley Perry was a 'half-breed' Nakoda and his wife Mary Haley was a 'half-breed' White Clay. There was always plenty of ammunition for a good debate. Charlie and Mary were the parents of Aunt Jeanette Warrior. Jeanette's husband, Rufus Warrior, was a rancher in Hays and a friend to our family. I have many of my mother's memories of how Rufus and all of the ranchers gathered at harvest time and went from farm to farm to harvest the hay. The stacks of hay looked like huge loaves of bread.

Dora Helgeson and my mother went on and on with memories as if they were yesterday – the family gardening and canning of dozens of Mason jars filled with assorted jellies, fruits, and vegetables…and 'moonshine'. After a long goodbye, exchange of recipes and one last Lucky Lager beer, we piled in the old worse for wear '48 Chevy Coupe and headed the eight miles to Percy and Gretchen's for the rest of the afternoon. We drove through Beaver Creek and on to Big Warm. Aunt Gretchen and my mother drank several cups of Lipton tea, sharing the gossip from town. Gretchen didn't get into town that often living way out there. Sooner or later, without much discussion, they started the cooking frenzy. The men visited telling wild stories about the great warriors. My brothers asserted their alcohol fogged manhood getting bucked off one of their mustang horses not yet broken. Percy laughed, knowing they were city slickers; maybe they rode a horse once a year. They drank Lucky Lager beer to comfort their wounded Lakota-Nakoda-White Clay pride.

Once they 'had their jag', bellies were full and all the stories were told, we said goodbye to Percy and Gretchen. The Chevy staggered into the twilight evening, finally stopping at an old log shack. This was where 'Colonel' Healy lived. He was the father of my mother's ex-husband, and he lived alone in his shack. He was a mean old man, and I stayed near my mother while we visited the old log house. The odor of kerosene invaded your senses, the dim light of his lamp cast a primordial glow in the room. The radiating dry heat and the smell of Jack pine from the wood stove, mixed with the kerosene is an olfactory memory that I can't describe in sufficient words. The old man looked like he had stepped a hundred years forward in time.

He was dressed in Levi pants shined with blackened filth. He wore a plaid flannel shirt with suspenders. His boot heels were worn bowlegged and his fingers and teeth were stained from tobacco. We stayed long enough to give him the canned goods that my mother brought him. The evening was getting late and the sun had gone down below the horizon.

Back at home, my Lakota preoperational attempt at accommodation and assimilation, the fine art of existing in this world, was shaped and skewed forever. I became aware of my world, grew accustomed to the five room mansion where we now lived, and I met my two most trusted white friends. There were few racial barriers on the north side. Billy Wayne Ragsdale was assertive and convincing; from thin air and wild imaginations we created weaponry to fight off savage Indians with 1855 Model Colt Revolving Carbines or Dragoon pistols that didn't need bullets. We fought the Indian Wars massacre by massacre. We were John Wayne and James Stewart fighting those blood-thirsty savages. We even had 007 science fiction laser technology in our imaginary war on the Lakota. No wonder the Lakota lost against such a brilliant mind as Billy's creative genius. I became somewhat intuitively aware that perhaps his facts might be deceiving.

It was a bright, sunny March afternoon in 1957. The KOJM radio blasted the news as the day began. I saw the fear roll over my mother's face. The radio said, "Black people in the south are rioting and marching…there are people dying." I wasn't sure what rioting meant but from the look on my mother's face, I could tell it was not good. That was the first time I was aware that something outside my world was amiss. Especially if you were a 'nigger' and that was not a good word. I got in trouble for shouting it at my sister and pointing my middle finger at her. I didn't have any idea who Jim Crow was, but if he was a 'Crow', he could not be trusted. The Jim Crow South was full of hatred for black people. Not the kind of hate they had for Indians, everybody knows the only good Indian is a dead Indian. Without black people, who would pick their cotton, who would raise their children and who would be left to kill?

Victor and I sat near the airport at the infamous "Big John's Coulee". The coulee overlooked the Milk River valley. We were drinking Lucky Lager beer, sipping on it as we puffed on the chenupa, my ceremonial pipe for pegi'. "Remember when we met?" Victor asked. "No…of course, you fuckin' idiot!" I replied. "I can't remember who won the fight," he reminisced. I laughed. "Guess it doesn't matter," he said. Victor and I were going to graduate from high school in a year. I had tried to drop out the year before, but my mother wouldn't let me. School was just not my thing. Victor Miller and I had known each other since 1957 when we moved to the five room mansion on the north side. Victor took to school right away; he was the best student. I have to admit he was pretty smart for a white kid. I never considered him white. I guess I never really noticed…he was my friend, my brother. We threw our empty cans out the window and popped another Lucky Lager from the case in the back seat of his military green '68 Rambler.

My brother Chic was friends with Billy's brother, Tom Ragsdale. They'd killed a deer a few days before, the same day I turned three years old. My mother dressed me in my only 'holy' jacket and sent me outside so she could clean the five room mansion. I meandered around the yard, taking inventory of my store-bought toys in the new tractor tire sandbox. I had helped my dad put the sandbox next to the dilapidated porch just outside the door. The dirty pothole water in the driveway pushed through the holes in my shoes. It was fascinating watching the patterns the dirt made when it was stirred into the standing water. The way it swirled, then clouded the water in a liquid explosion. Chic grabbed me and took me to Tom's house. Billy and Raymond were Tom's little brothers and we played Buck Rogers outside while Tom and Chic butchered the deer. I had no clue who Buck Rogers was – we didn't have a television, but Billy had a grey and black tin toy spaceship and a ray-gun he got for Christmas.

I looked up from the Ragsdale's mud puddle, and there was Billy with another 'pink' kid coming down the alley from Billy's ranch. The alley was two tire tracks overgrown with weeds. The challenge was getting past Eddy Hilderman's Rottweilers. Even with them behind a six-foot-high chicken wire fence, the sight of their teeth and the sound of their vicious bark sent terror through a three-year-old. The ranch was a rundown house and barn that had received no maintenance since they were built. There was an add-on plywood bathroom and bedroom. The leaning two stall garage was filled with musty leather saddles and bridles, and greasy tools covered a homemade bench leaning the opposite direction. The yard was filled with milkweed two or three feet high. There were signs of a lawn at one time, probably around the turn of the 20th century. It was better than our house. You could shit in a toilet that flushed inside the house, out of the cold.

My father knew Slim, he was Billy's father and everyone else knew Slim too. He proudly admired the house as his five-acre gentleman's ranch. He was from the Oklahoma hills and drawled when he talked. In actuality Slim didn't have a pot to piss in. He worked his wife Freda like a dog; she worked for the Harlem News five days a week. His daughter Peggy delivered groceries for the Merry Market after school. Slim constantly bragged about his oldest son, Bob Ragsdale – he was a famous real life cowboy. Slim bragged, "He just won the 1957 World Champion Calf Roping in Chowchilla, California." He may as well have said my son's the best calf-roper in the whole world…that makes me better than you. My father shrugged his shoulders and went about his way. Slim pulled his straw cowboy hat down over his eyes, demonstrating his white Cherokee superiority. It was a convenience when it benefitted him, but he showed no sign of being Indian other than his poverty. He hoped that his son's success elevated his status.

Billy and the new kid came closer. I came to an abrupt stop, feeling a sense of betrayal. We were best friends yesterday. As they approached, I heard them ponder how fun it would be to swim in the irrigation ditch. The ditch ran along the graveled Highway 241 north to the white towns of Turner and Hogeland near the Canadian border. Billy's friend was quite an orator. He convinced Billy that it wasn't going to be a good ending if his father caught him. I asked this new kid what his name was and who made him boss. With authority he assured me, "My name is Vic." I was sure that this kid was attempting to deceive me. The scuffle was on to the death, rolling in the north-side dirt, scrapping like Custer and Sitting Bull through mud puddles and into the dirty ditch water. He was Sitting Bull and I was John Wayne. Bill, Vic and me…we were inseparable after that.

We fought every Indian War shown on the Grande Theater cinematic screen. We fought bravely with John Wayne, Jimmy Stewart and Glenn Ford. Billy, Vic and me…heroes in our own childhood imaginations. I always insisted on being John Wayne to fight the Indians. John Wayne never lost and he never ran out of bullets killing those evil Lakota savages. My nephew Jerry evened the score when he came from Helena during the summers. One year he came to live with us for most of the school year. He'd already seen all the new movies, so we acted out all the scenes, including the hangings. Jerry and Victor tried to hang me, but they weren't strong enough to get me off the ground, even when I stood on my tiptoes. Vic always handed over his store bought, shiny, pearl-handled cap guns so I could shoot him dead over and over in those deadly gunfights. That was where Vic learned empathy for the 'red man'. That's where I learned to shoot Indians.

Vic lived across the street from me in a big pink house. It had an outhouse in back with a quarter moon on the door. Billy and Vic lived across the alley from each other. Our world grew with age. School opened up my understanding like a Hiroshima mushroom cloud. I spent much of my time protecting Vic from the White Clay-Nakoda Indian kids who wanted to beat him up, I guess because he was different than us. My cousin, Waynie, was determined to catch him alone because he was angry about being poor. Vic was an easy target since he would rather talk than fight. My nephew, Jerry, lived with us in third grade, before he was sent to reform school. We were walking home after school when Waynie caught Victor just as he crossed the railroad tracks. He was hitting and kicking Victor to the ground. Victor's books dropped, and still he wouldn't fight back. Jerry had fast shoes and he caught Waynie easily; Jerry had lots of practice outrunning white kids and cops in Helena. We gave Waynie his due. After that nobody picked on Vic except me. He was my brother.

Chapter 11

Black and White Proof

Unfortunately, being the next oldest, Barbara was responsible for managing me and the herd of younger 'three eighths-breed' nephews and nieces in our family. My sister was eight years older than me. She had the gift of music; she played guitar and sang ever since I could remember. When she opened her mouth, you swore the heavens opened up and an angel had started to sing. Most of my 'Heinz 57' Indian family had musical gifts. Unfortunately, they took all the talent and there was none left for me, the youngest. And when my cousins, Carol Dean Gladeau or Carol Belt joined in, you would swear that there was a chorus of angels singing *Honky Tonk Angels* or *Crazy*. Katie Wells and Patsy Cline would have been proud. Indian girls sang with soul – white girls sang the notes. There were never many Indian girls in school chorus, so my sister didn't last long. They were jealous.

Barbara's teens were cut short when she got pregnant at 15 years old; my sister kept her head up high and didn't shed a tear, not in public anyway. She had no choice – she was taken from home by the welfare lady. The Montana State Welfare Department forced her to go away to the unwed mothers' home in Helena. When she came home in the spring, she had a baby. His name was George Timothy. She named him after our grandfather and our brother who died of polio back in the '30s. She married an angry white man when she was 16 years old. Like my mother, she and her child took the beatings for the mistake of being half-breed Indians.

The little yellow Philco radio was our connection to the outside world. KOJM radio blasted during the waking hours. They broadcast the local *Mayda McCarney Hour*, local news and, a few times a day, the world news. My mother drank Lipton tea, listened to the radio and worried. In the '60s there were a lot of worries around the world. She was fearful of the white man authority. She had experienced the wrath in the boarding schools. It was beat into her that Catholicism was the road to Jesus and an imaginary kingdom called heaven. The civil rights tension and frustrations of black people escalated to violence. A man named Martin Luther King talked about racism, oppression and discrimination. In the news of the day, the Freedom Riders were killed in the south. They were trouble makers who disappeared in the middle of the night, never to be seen again. There was only talk that they had left town in the middle of the night. When they were found dead, my mother worried for her sons who were out in the world. They were naïve and ignorant to the dangers that loomed. Even in our little world of Harlem, Montana, Indian boys were found beaten, left along country roads.

Gordon Azure was one of our many distant cousins, but I wasn't sure how we were related. He and my brother Ron were friends. My sister Annette called Ron 'Byo' when he was a baby, and it stuck. Gordon and Byo were good friends in school until Byo dropped out his sophomore year. He joined the U.S. Army to emulate our brother Marvin. Gordon's older sisters were Pearl,

Ione and Ruby. They were close in age and friends with my sister Annette. Annette led them astray with her fascination for ex-convicts and 'bad boys'. Her friends Blue, Tiny and Bitsy Bear were not to be messed with either, and the macho teenage boys were leery of humiliation from the girls. The Azure and Bear girls were tougher than the toughest girls in *Westside Story*, all of them hardened by the reservation. It was expected of Indian girls to stick together. The white girls feared and hated them secretly behind their backs.

Gordon's younger brother, Pockets, hung out with my brother Chic and Bobby Shafer. Bobby had a car. The Indian girls were impressed with his rusted out '38 Chevy. There was only a driver's seat plus a couple of five-gallon cans to sit on if you could manage the corners. Bobby and Chic were never as cool as Gordon and Byo. The older boys wore their hair in duck tails and dressed like they had walked out of a James Dean movie – white tee shirts and blue jeans with the cuffs turned up. Not wide cuffs like the dirt farmer kids, but just one narrow turn for effect. The white kids looked like Richie Cunningham or Ralph Malph stereotypes. They passed by the five room mansion on Highway 241. Victor was related to a lot of them in one way or another, by marriage, or maybe a cousin once or twice removed.

Gordon's little brother, Alan, was my sister Barbara's age. They were born after the war in 1946. Alan teased my sister without mercy. I enjoyed it because she always made my life miserable. Alan was a miniature Gordon, with an Azure sense of humor and a rebellious nature. The final touch was the penny loafer shoes, loaded with two shiny silver dimes for the fashionable '50s Indian ghetto hood look. They lived on the north side, across 30 Mile Creek. They were a step above on the Indian social ladder. They had a car that Gordon always worked on; the starter or generator was often the problem, sometimes a radiator or dirt in the fuel line.

Their big sister, Anna Lee, was married to a white man, George Fetter. They lived on the north side, too. Their kids, Junior, Eddy and Franky, were around my age. Junior was the oldest, and Tony was the baby in smelly diapers. I was never allowed to go to their house, but they came to our house sometimes with their mom. Integration crept across the American south by force, but not in spirit. Integration also crept across Harlem to the north side. Our family assimilated with the other unworthy poor who lived on the north side along with the other Indian families. We were to blame for our own damned social disposition. There were also white families who fancied themselves as landowners. There were the Seimans, Swendsides and the Ragsdales; we all knew they were better than us. Both the Indians and the white people knew who was superior – there was no debate. Being white poor isn't much better than being Indian poor, except if you are white you have a pretty good disguise. It's hard to tell a poor white from a rich white except for the clothes, unless you are a person of wealth. When you are white, people don't look at you like you are going to take their scalp, rape their daughter or kill their dog. White people look at white people and see the American flag.

All my half-brothers and sisters were so unaware of this Lakota dilemma, I couldn't believe they didn't notice, didn't seem to care. I could feel the stares of the white people when I went to the Merry Market with my mother. Their thoughts were visible in their facial expressions. I could almost hear what they thought about me and my dirt poor mother as they looked on with superficial compassion and pity. One Christmas the Lion's Club gave me a homemade sled. I broke my leg trying to negotiate the curve sledding at the 30 Mile Creek bridge. I learned not to take gifts from white people…they couldn't be trusted. They always came with a price. My family went along as if everything was okay. They pretended that discrimination and prejudice didn't exist. We struggled along in abject poverty, but still racism wasn't targeting Indian people; the intent was to keep those 'niggers' in their place. We just had to suffer along with them.

Chic occasionally took me with him and his best friend, Bobby Schaefer. Bobby had an old Chevy they drove on the back roads hunting deer, pheasant or rabbits. My brother's real name was Franklin Alan, but everybody knew him as Chic. It was pretty obvious when Fred Hutchins came to visit one summer. Chic's twin was Alan Franklin 'Chuck' Healy. Chuck was his spitting image and his head bobbled like a dashboard ornament when he walked. My mother had an affair with her sister's brother-in-law, Fred. It was a wartime affair that was brief, leaving my mother pregnant to face Bud Healy after the war ended. Meanwhile he fathered another dozen illegitimate Healy children, drinking his demons to the grave. I speculated my mom was far ahead of Gloria Steinem and Jane Fonda's women's lib feminist movement.

Neither the twins nor my mother were ever forgiven. It angered Bud Healy and the beatings increased. Chuck was a 'nervous child'. The chaos of an alcoholic family was too much trauma; he needed to be in a calm environment. There was no calm environment living in fear, never knowing when Bud would come home drunk and the beatings would begin. The white doctor at the Fort Belknap hospital told Mayme that the child needed to be raised alone without his brothers and sisters. My mother tearfully gave him to Frank and Julia. They took him and raised him in a town called Dillon. Chic went on the bus every summer to visit him. I don't think he liked being under Aunt Sis's charge; he was always anxious to get home to his friends and our poverty. The twins had genetics in common, that was about it. Chic learned empathy; his brother learned selfishness.

When school started, Beatrice Doney and Leonard Pronto moved in next door. Their son, Johnny Wayne, was in first grade.

His sister, Ruby, was my age; we weren't old enough to go to school yet. They lived in the house where Franky Stiffarm and Violet Shields lived the year before. Violet was my sister-in-law Joan's mother. Joan was married to my brother, Babe. The house had a small kitchen, a main room and a bedroom. The kitchen had a small four burner gas stove, but only two of them worked. It also had an apple box frost box set into a small window frame that was badly in need of paint and repair. The worn linoleum was peeling and the pink paint was chipping off the wallpaper underneath. Beatrice and Leonard moved in with their two kids, Johnny Wayne and Ruby. Beatrice was a young woman and Leonard was friends with my brother, Jimmy. They drank together with Leonard's brother, Gene. Jimmy had the demons of Bud Healy in him. He was cowardly, filled with hate and just plain mean. Once when my father passed out, Jimmy stole $740, his three-month paycheck. There was evidence of his deed, but Jimmy denied it on a stack of bibles.

Johnny Wayne Doney was easy to get along with, but he spent most of his time in Zortman with his cousin, Kenny. Kenny was a bully for a scrawny little guy – you had to be a bully to survive on the reservation. Ruby spent a lot of time at our house with her mom during the long, hot summer. Beatrice was friends with my sister Annette's crew, and she was also friends with my mom, so she was a familiar face at our house. She and my mother used to sit and gossip, drinking Lipton iced tea. They always laughed, joking at some Indian foolishness. Ruby and I played in the tractor tire sandbox. We imagined a world of white privilege neither of us ever knew. We drove my plastic toy car in the dirt; it had two hard plastic models of a man and woman inside. We imagined it was Ruby beside me and we were going on a trip. She was a mom and I was a dad, and we scolded our imaginary children. Ruby moved to another house; she went away in third grade. She said she was going to come back, but I never saw her again.

Jimmy and Bernice moved into the house next door when the Doneys moved out. They had been together three years and had three kids already. They were married in the Blaine County Jail after being arrested for public drunkenness. They got the spirit right there in jail; they saw God, they saw the light…Halleluiah be to Gawd! Once they were out of jail, they were back to drinking. They totaled their beat-up Ford and got a $10,000 settlement. My mother took care of their kids when they were drunk and hung over. It was the warped family pattern of Native American tradition. Indian grandparents cared for the grandchildren when the men were off hunting or the women gathering berries. The pattern morphed to alcoholic behaviors; grandparents love their grandchildren, enabling parents to continue drinking. My mother was stuck in another cycle of codependence. Jimmy and Bernice took advantage of her help while they abused and neglected their children, giving them F.I. Muscatel to put them to sleep at night.

My brother Chic left home when he was 16 years old to join the U.S. Navy. All of our older brothers were in the military; it was an escape from poverty and the grip of the reservation. Babe and Byo were in the U.S. Army. Jimmy tried to make a go of it in the U.S. Air Force, but he got a dishonorable discharge after a year – the alcohol demon was too strong. I wrote to Chic in San Diego; he was stationed there most of the time he was in the Navy. We were happy to see him when he came home after basic training. He told me stories about his fame as a heroic diver. Every year he sent my mother books filled with pictures of his adventures as black and white proof. Chic never was one to stay away from home for very long. He had the thumb and the demeanor for travel when he put on his hitchhiking shoes. One year he made it home from San Diego to Harlem in less than 24 hours for Dodson Fair. He came home on leave and forgot to go back when he was supposed to. He got in trouble for being A.W.O.L. and got sent to the brig for a month.

We sat in the old '48 Chevy coupe by the Chevron garage next to the 'money tree' where the winos slept. Occasionally they dropped loose change from their pockets in their shameless sleep. Chic flirted with my sister's friend, Kathy Woods. She shrieked his name, alerting Jim Pollard, the Chief of Police. Since Chic was A.W.O.L., there was an order issued by the Navy for his arrest and incarceration. Chief Pollard had to arrest him even though he liked Chic. He didn't have any choice. My mother begged and pleaded, bargaining that she would send him back to San Diego on the Greyhound the following Monday. Chief Pollard apologized profusely as he booked Chic at the Harlem police station, and the iron door of the jail cell closed behind him. I went with my mother to see him. It was the first time I had ever seen anyone locked up in a jail cell. Chic had never been in jail, and he bravely promised Mom he would be okay. Mr. Pollard felt bad, and he tried to get my mother to understand, but she would hear nothing of his unreasonable deed.

My father took my mom to the New England Bar to calm her down, she was so filled with anguish. It was the only time I ever saw my mother drunk. She was snockered, blitzed, shitfaced drunk. She saw Chief Pollard in front of the bar and attacked him with a carton of Pall Mall cigarettes. She fell off the sidewalk, still shouting obscenities at him as she fell hard to the concrete. My dad helped her from the ground and brought her home in Jim Harvey's taxi. He helped her to bed in her drunken condition. She was still fighting Mr. Pollard, wanting to get back to the jail. As she flailed, she threw her purse, scattering change around the room and under the bed. My nephew Jerry and I scrambled in search of the scattered change. With flashlights guiding our childish Lakota-Chippewa-White Clay fingers, we gathered the treasure of nickels, dimes, quarters and shiny half-dollar coins.

The following day my nephew Jerry and I had a grand ol' time at Don's Pharmacy. There were so many choices. We spent the morning buying comic books, toys and roasted cashews from the heated turntable behind the counter. There was even enough money left over to have a burger, fries and Coke at Merle's Confectionary. We still had a handful of change, so we went to Parnell's Jewelry and the Five and Dime store across the street to spend the rest of the evidence. My mother couldn't use her arm for days after her injury. Annette woke the next day, full of energy. Mom was in pain mentally and physically, and her spirit wasn't that bright either. She tried to reach the top shelf for the Folgers coffee. Grimacing in pain, both her shoulder and ego were bruised by her disdainful episode. My sister cheered her on and glorified her aggressive behavior.

Chic returned to San Diego to face his A.W.O.L. offense, but he was home a few months later. He caught a ride with a trucker all the way from San Diego. The driver bought him breakfast and dinner along the way. This time he went back when he was supposed to. He was not fond of jails after his time in the brig. Once he was discharged from the Navy, Chic returned home permanently. He had married a young girl named Kathy Oshio. She fell for his boyish smile, simplicity and boy scout personality. He brought her home in 1964 all the way from California; he told her they were going to live in a teepee on the reservation. She didn't seem to like our five room mansion. Although we did our best to make her feel welcome, I think the poverty and the outhouse were too much for her to handle. She wasn't with us long before she found a man of means in Malta, and that was the last we ever saw of her.

Chapter 12

Idiopathic Broken Lakota Dreams

As the '50s concluded in a swirl of imaginary Wild West and World War II adventures, Victor Miller and I were friends, closer than brothers. Victor was a practical, pragmatic and Socratic thinker. He analyzed and researched outcomes. His entrepreneurial savvy was fascinating. He was saving for old age by the time we reached second grade. His grandpa and dad helped him start his sheep business raising bum lambs. He sold the wool at the Blaine County Fair and the sheep at auction. The money was deposited in his bank account. He was encouraged by watching his savings grow over the years. I, on the other hand, had the buffalo spirit in my soul and accepted most challenges in a thoughtless heartbeat. Who knew if tomorrow might ever come? I was determined to live life as it happened. I tried saving my last dollar, but always donated it for Lucky Lager beer or the next lid of pegi'.

In August, 1960, we entered the academia of 'Dick and Jane'. Billy, Victor and I anxiously discussed the adventure of going to school with all the other kids while we waited for the school bell to ring. We were bonded together in poverty, victims sentenced to a life on the north side, beyond the Burlington Northern Railroad tracks where most of my rich Chippewa cousins lived. We lived across 30 Mile Creek where the winos gathered to drink their wine and 'have their way' with their wino women. We lived by the little brown house where Billy's Aunt Ester lived with her mentally ill son, Ronny, who talked to spoons. Victor's house was the pink house, the second house to the right, next to Brother Bear's house. Brother was mentally retarded, and he was a bully, probably because he was picked on for his mental deficits which only made him meaner.

Billy's home was his father Slim's 'ranch', also the home of Billy's oldest brother, Bob Ragsdale, the rodeo hero of the far north side. Billy was stuck in the middle between having to outmaneuver his older brother Tom and being the scapegoat for his mischievous little brother, Raymond, who was the spitting image of Slim. Little Raymond was never victim to the lariat. Billy's mother Freda was his saving grace and protector. Billy seemed to be Slim's source of anger because he didn't want anything to do with horses or being a cowboy. His mother was a kind practical and gentle woman with a radiant spirit dulled by her years with Slim. He was a mean and gruff man in his early 50s, tall with a craggy Cherokee face. He was one of my father's friends when Slim was in his rare drinking mood.

As the fall progressed to September, leaves fell from the trees to die in the streets along with our innocence. Billy, Victor and I entered Lincoln Grade School for the first time. Billy and Victor were the only kids I knew other than Donald Shawl. We were immediately separated in the world of white academia. It was my first personal encounter with an authoritarian bureaucratic institution, and there was no choice in the matter. We were separated by our academic level of intelligence and, of course, by race. The white yellow-haired man in charge asserted in so many words, "You smart white kids in this line; you dumb white kids in this line; you dumb Indian White Clay-Nakodas in this line, and the rest of you really stupid losers and Lakotas in this line." White kids to the right, White Clay kids to the left, Lakota kids…just plain wrong.

I was unaware, didn't even suspect that we were poor until I started school. I grew up in extreme chaos, poverty and alcoholic dysfunction, and that was a normal day. Everywhere I looked, all of the white kids had shiny new stuff and new clothes to wear to school every day. They had shoes without holes in the bottoms by the time spring came. I tried to use cardboard cutouts to keep the rocks out. When the cardboard got wet in the slushy snow, it turned to giant spit-wads in my shoes. I think my first inkling life had gone awry was when I had to go to the special line for lunch. The white woman told me that was where the poor kids had to line up for our daily USDA government approved humiliation.

Victor's father, Jay, was a Korean War veteran like my oldest brother, Babe. Only he didn't carry his anger around him like Babe did, always looking for a fight. Jay was a gregarious man with a charismatic personality, always with a joke to tell. Jay's father was Grampa Clyde. He was a shiny-headed bald man, gruff in character but soft with kindness. He always came to thaw the water pipes in our five room mansion. There was no insulation on the pipes coming out of the ground. When it got really cold they froze solid. My mom kept the water dripping, but sometimes there was a hard freeze during the night. Clyde was married to Gramma Sarah at one time, and now they lived across the street from one another at the end of the block. Victor's Gramma Sarah Miller was our landlord. She owned the dilapidated mansion we lived in and the one next door where Violet and Frankie, Beatrice and Leonard, and

Jimmy and Bernice had lived. My cousin, Monty, and Francis lived there now.

Francis had two daughters, Virginia Parish and Susie Belgard. Virginia was in my grade; she was a tall pretty girl, light in complexion. Susie was darker in coloring, more like her mother. Monty worked odd jobs – seasonal work was mostly what Indians were suited for in those days. It was unheard of for an Indian to have a job other than the kind of menial work available to migrant Mexican workers. Carpentry and horseshoeing were our family trades, but there wasn't much need for horseshoers. Carpentry was good work when you could get it. The Brekkes, the Yeomans and ol' Paul Miller had the construction business sewn up. If you were able to find their good grace, perhaps they would give you a part time job, mostly doing the dirty clean-up work. It was demeaning for a skilled carpenter, but at least it was work. The drinking habit preoccupied Monty and Francis's priorities. Without notice, Virginia and Susie were gone from school. They moved to Helena, we heard.

Victor's Gramma Sarah worked at the Coast to Coast hardware store. Elmer and Charlotte Nelson were the owners. He taught Sunday school at the EUB (Evangelical United Brethren) church. Elmer was my Sunday school teacher on one of the several attempts I made trying to understand the whiteman's God. Besides, they had the best Halloween parties. Sarah was an independent woman like my mom. She didn't drive and walked everywhere she went. I went to her house once with Victor, and she gave us cookies and lemonade. She was nice because I was friends with Victor, I supposed. She frequented Victor's house for Sunday dinners. She wasn't Jay's mother, but she had raised him since he was a small boy. The family accepted her as their grandma, and she accepted the responsibility. She didn't drink; she provided stability for

Victor's family. She babysat when Jay and Alice were at the VFW club until Victor took over the job when he was ten years old.

Things were a little different at my house. Times like Christmas were mostly filled with my father's futile effort to hide the fact that he was Lakota. I was aware we were savages in the movies, I just didn't know that's the way white people really felt about us. When my dad was intoxicated and filled with his Lakota shame, he would say, "You ain't a man until you pull yourself up by your boot straps." Although I was quite enough aware to internalize his shame, I begged my mother, hoping for a pair of boots. I never got them. The $35 welfare check never went far enough for her to buy boots, and the money my father earned went mostly for Lucky Lager beer and Seagram's 7 medication. I often feared the thought that I would never be a 'man' with bootstraps. The pair of shoes I wore had holes in the bottom. By spring the freezing water got pretty cold…sort of like my relationship with my father. He never talked to me. I tried but didn't have a whole lot of expectations.

By the next year my world view and perception of life shifted to the left like a great metaphysical tsunami. I was ten years old and anticipating the excitement of Christmas, even though I knew there was no Santa Clause and there would be no gifts. I got in trouble for stealing an old timer butcher knife and towel set for my mother, and she made me take them back. I had nothing to give my mother, brother, sister or anyone else. My father came through the door smelling of Seagram's 7 and delirious with his World War II memories. He came in the room to argue with my mother, and he fell left, into the Christmas tree, tipping it over, off the army blanket-covered table where it was perched. I could hear the fragile glass bulbs break as the tree hit the floor. The lights went dark, and that was the last time I participated in this 'waste of my time'. "Jesus, my ass…God is full of shit!" I thought to myself. My mother wept her quiet Lakota tears in private so I couldn't see her, but I could hear her. I still heard her as the KOJM broadcast of the midnight mass played on the Philco radio.

My mother was a woman of great faith. The next day my cousin Buddy showed up in the frozen morning. He gave my mother $500 to keep for him, asking her not to give it to him if he was drunk. He was akin to shifty doin's, but she agreed though unsure if it was legally gotten gain. He knew his fortune was more secure in my mother's possession than in Fort Knox. Buddy often stayed with us when he was down and out or had a hangover and was hungry. That Christmas day he also brought with him a huge 25-pound turkey, two bags of groceries and several shiny colored packages for my brother, sister and me. My mom gave Buddy a hug around his neck, "I didn't know what I was going to do…I'm out of everything. I was just trying to figure out what to make for breakfast…are you going to stay? There's coffee on the heater…I'll get you a cup." Mom put away the groceries, set the turkey near the heater to thaw and gave thanks.

I watched my father withdraw into himself; he worked and drank himself to death. It was an insidious progression to the grave. He was never around; he was lost in his own thoughts. He spent years in isolated solitude making white men wealthy, raising their crops and cattle. I always thought that he was quite generous as he bought gifts for his boss's sons. They reminded me over the years what a good guy he was, the horses and trucks he bought them. They genuinely reminisced what a good man he was, and I believed them. I asked him for a .22 once; it cost $20 at Elmer Nelson's Coast to Coast store. It was no horse or truck, maybe not even what I was worth. I'm sure he would have preferred a white son. I screamed from the corners of the universe; I did everything I could to communicate with him, but still he never heard me.

I saw every movie that came to the Grand Theater in Harlem. My dad's momentary visits always involved having me go to the movies so I was occupied elsewhere. Later on there were years he didn't show up for Christmas. This was all part of my native training for no emotional access. This pattern was beat into my dad and his father before him. Now it is generationally handed down while children watch feet pass from their quiet corner and listen intently to their role models' intimations of morality.

On the rare occasions when my father returned home, he was in retreat from his alcoholic binges. My mom loved him in spite of his absence and nursed him back to health after his nocturnal terrors. She was just happy having him home. She hummed a random tune from the '30s and busied herself making his favorite meals. After he was coherent, he gave me explicit instructions and a $5 bill with the picture of Abraham Lincoln on it. My task was to walk to Don's Pharmacy to get him five packs of filter-less Pall Mall cigarettes, a $1 assortment of five-cent candy bars and a stag magazine with tales that claimed to be true stories of macho adventures. On the slow half-mile walk home, I read fantastic stories of scantily clad women in Nazi distress. I wondered about the lives of those heroic people on the magazine covers and the 'fine art' on the pages inside. When I got home my dad counted the twenty-five-cent candy bars and gave me my choice for the effort. I had earned his good grace for the day.

It was a chilly and drizzling day, but my mother was determined to get to the Merry Market as all the cupboards were bare. The 'slow elk' in the antique Philco freezer was gone. The Merry Market had a colorful assortment of penny candy. I knew Mary O'Brien or Mary Calvert would not be able to resist my pitiful Lakota eyes; they always gave me a piece of the gooey colored penny candy and pinched my fat cheeks. I didn't have a choice, I tagged along with my mother as she frugally selected the cheapest items on the wooden shelves. She took her meager purchases to the checkout knowing she could create a masterpiece of fine Lakota cuisine. Bean soup and frybread was a specialty. The end of the month was when she made the best stuff. Wheel bread was for the last day of the month when there was nothing left but commodity flour dust.

Mary Calvert checked out the groceries at the cash register stand. I stood quietly by my mother's side, looking pitifully at Mary…then at the candy. She graciously gave me permission to have a cinnamon bear if I helped my mother carry the groceries. We left the store, walked past Gambles, and across the street past Parnell's Five and Dime store. We crossed Highway 2 to the local Chevron gas station where we picked up a tire patch kit for Jimmy. As we passed the Chuckwagon Café, the odor of hamburger and onions frying wafted off the grill. Several businessmen in suits and straw fedora hats walked toward the door. My mother hurried past, practically dragging me and the small sack of groceries I carried. She explained the white people didn't want Indians in their café. We weren't good enough, besides we couldn't afford to eat their fancy food. For a Lakota-Chippewa, racial prejudice and discrimination became just another guaranteed expectation.

I never knew my oldest brother when I was a kid. Marvin was 22 years older than me. I came to dread when he came home on leave from the army. He married Joan Shields in 1956 when she wasn't more than a child herself. On their wedding night after a night of drinking, she rode my tricycle around our living room. Marvin's nickname was Babe, and he fancied himself as a fighter. His U.S. Army photo was placed in a prominent place on my mother's dresser. I was taught to pay reverent homage to his picture. He looked grown up in his U.S. Army uniform. He sent home $40 allotment checks to my mother; it was taken out of his army pay every month. She saved the allotment checks until he came home.

He wasn't home for more than a few days, already asking her for money till he got his paycheck. Without fail, she dragged out the stack of checks, signed them and turned them over to him so he would have money to drink on.

The visits from Babe and Joan weren't often, but it was quite memorable when they did come home. One time they came from California, the next time they came from Georgia. Their oldest son, Marvin Jr., was born at Ford Ord. They were gone a couple years to Germany where their youngest son, Brian, was born. When they did come home it upset the homeostasis of our dysfunctional routines. A few times brother Byo came home on leave from the army at the same time. Byo was five years younger than Babe. They both played guitar; Byo was naturally gifted while Babe struggled to make the notes. When they were home together, the visits usually started with a family feast that was in perpetual preparation for days. It was a Lakota tradition my mother learned from First Holy Woman and her mother, Julia. The festivities started out with a carefree welcome home from all the 'cousints' with plenty of Lucky Lager beer and happy banter between the macho young men. Those were the days of Ferlin Husky, Marty Robbins and Roy Acuff. Babe and Byo got out their prized Gibson guitars they bought in their worldly U.S. Army adventures. It wasn't long before more teenager cousins and friends started to show up for food and festivities. The Lucky Lager beer flowed gently at first and then into a rapid white-water stream of cursing and accusations. The evening ended abruptly in a crescendo of drinking and determination to get to Beanie's Tavern for the impending fight between the Lakota and the White Clay. The fight usually started by midnight with one of the Cole boys flirting with Joan. She egged it on until Babe's jealousy was at a fury. There was always one more advance from Winky Cole before fists started flying.

This time it turned into a regular family reunion; I'd never seen my brothers and sisters all together. The rare occasion that Babe, Byo and Annette were home at the same time was a novelty I had never experienced. About 3:00 a.m., the night was broken with screams and loud cursing throughout the house. Babe got a gun from the baby crib where his son Marvin Jr. was sleeping. He took the gun and headed out the door, telling Mom he was going to kill Annette. My mother grabbed him before he was able to escape in the dark. She told him if he was going to shoot anybody he had to go through her. The gun was loaded and he pointed it in my mother's stomach. It was by grace it didn't go off. Barbara ran across to the Swendside's house and called the cops. My mother wrestled the gun from my brother's intoxicated hands and told me to go throw it in the weeds. I took the gun and threw it behind the fifty-gallon trash cans in the waist high overgrowth. Jim Pollard came and took Babe to jail for the night until he was sober.

The next morning Annette and her boyfriend, Laramie, loaded up their '52 Ford Victoria. Scolding her kids Jerry and Doll to hurry, they left back to Helena without explanation. My mother had just started kneading the dough to make bread when Babe came through the door. There was blood on his clothes and his face was swollen; his hair was matted with dried blood. He was sober and apparently had the 'pissed off' beaten out of him. He told us Annette had hit him over the head with a full bottle of Orange Crush soda pop, the bottle shattering to pieces. My mother dropped her task and went to work co-dependently cleaning and patching his wounds for another round. There were small shards of glass embedded in his scalp. The lump on the back of his head was about three inches in diameter with a half inch raised contusion on the side where he landed on the bar stool railing. Within a day he was ready to go back to the bar for another attempt at the Coles. It was just another lesson he never learned.

I came home from school to find my mother with red eyes from crying. Immediately thinking that something was wrong with someone in our family, my thoughts were of Boyd. Mom had just heard on the radio that Martin Luther King had been killed. All I knew about him was that he was a black Negro man. He talked about being free and having a dream. It was in our Weekly Reader at school last week. "Shit…dreams are for white people; the Lakota-Chippewa always get fucked over." I had learned that in school…" Those fuckin' Injuns," I laughed to myself.

We were the savages and they were the civilized people according to those fuckin' history books. Whose history were they talking about? The stuff we learned by patriotic indoctrination made no sense to us. This wasn't my country. This was a country for the white people on the south side who bought this crap. Of the rich people, by the rich people, and for the rich people. There were no dreams for Indians, only *red shadow* nightmares passed from generation to generation.

It was usually the middle of the night when my brother Babe showed up at the door, stinking of alcohol and routinely beat to a bloody pulp. He fought the air when it blew too hard. I think he was fighting his father. Mr. Healy was the reason for Babe leaving home to go to the Korean War. My mother told me Babe went to the U.S. Army when he was only 15 years old. She said he told her that if she did not sign the U.S. Government paper for him to join, he was going to kill his father for beating her, beating him and taking his rage out on them. My mother said she cried because neither choice was good. She could either lose her son to the Korean War or to the White Man prison that promised by law to take him away.

Chapter 13

Knee High by the Fourth of July

Grandpa Clyde owned a farm across the road from Victor's big pink mansion. It was a short walk along 30 Mile Creek and through a field of weeds to the dairy's milk house. The dairy was Clyde's source of income, and it was a relatively good one. He wasn't rich, but he was able to help Jay buy his house when he returned from his adventure in Alaska. That was back when I first met Victor a few years before. We worked for his grandpa together, learning Mexican cuss words from Johnny Rodriguez. Hell, all I knew about my grandparents was from a box of pictures and stories I heard from my family. The stories were my family inheritance, but they didn't help us buy a house. I doubt my father would ever have done anything like that; it would take responsibility and anyway, he was never home. Besides, he wouldn't have wanted to go talk to the white banker who couldn't wait to tell him no.

Victor's other grandpa, Dan Hay, was the Blaine County Sheriff. He was Alice's dad and an important man. Vic repeated his grandpa's stories over and over, stories about his grandpa catching murderin' thieves. There was that one Hollister murder case that he never could solve; Grandpa Dan still thought about that one, I was assured. Hollister must have been a really bad man. I felt bad for Vic's grandpa. I liked him – he was always good to me and my mother.

Dan and my mother were close in age. He was a young Scotchman and a well-known 'horse thief'. He tried to steal one of my grandfather George's best Lakota-Kootenai horses. Mom told her story with a smile, doing her best to keep a straight face. She occasionally chuckled to herself while telling how she chased him down and gave him a thrashing with her 'chain quirt' that she used to discipline her unruly Lakota steed. They never discussed how they knew each other. Dan was always very respectful and kind to her. He was like a grandpa to me, and he gave me fatherly advice and praise, just like he did with his grandsons.

Dan's wife, Edna, was a kind, inconspicuous woman; she survived the depression and was quite industrious. Dan and Edna lived in Chinook, the county seat. Blaine County is where the ghosts of Chief Joseph's people walk the earth. It was obvious that Victor and his grandma had a special bond. She gave him the attention that Alice couldn't. Alice loved to yell; she could raise the dead with her sarcasm and sharp-tongued personality. Jay and Alice were one of my adopted families during my youthful search for my Lakota-Chippewa sanity and my very own pair of boots. Alice joked about me being a 'Chippi" and that I should be getting treaty money soon. It was mostly annoying but she thought it was funny, so I just took it knowing she never meant any harm. They were by no means a perfect family but compared to my family, they had survived fairly well. All I saw in my family was despair and failure. Our legacy had no bright sides or success stories. Every Indian story is a sad story.

Victor and I were on our way to the milk house at Grandpa Clyde's to do our early morning chores. One of the dying trees along the weedy path had to be chopped down. By then Victor had retrieved his hunting knife and hatchet from my sister. Barbara had confiscated his weapons when he and Raleigh Brockie tried to scalp me. Every week Victor, Billy and I used the hatchet to build our forts along 30 Mile Creek. The pitiful tree was targeted for termination, the decision was made, and there was no turning back. Victor sharpened the implements on the 100-year-old grinding stone in the Ragsdale yard. We were sophisticated for ten year olds, planning our task and scheduling our plan. Victor's Cub Scout book was our guide; he wore his neckerchief and Cub Scout hat for the commencement of D-Day.

We worked for days chopping through the sorrowful Aspen tree marked for certain demise. Victor hid the knife and hatchet near the creek bank, not to be discovered. He tried to direct the project like the pictures in the book. We took turns with the knife and hatchet, whittling away on both sides of the tree. The long week passed, and finally the tree fell. We saw it begin to waver and quiver with the final blows of the hatchet. It was leaning the wrong direction. I pushed with all of my 180 pounds, but it didn't budge – it leaned further. We heard the snapping of wood fibers as it came crashing down in front of us. The tree fell across the road, blocking the milk truck's entrance to the dairy. We hesitantly announced to Grandpa Clyde that we had finished cutting down the dying Aspen. He was instantly animated. His face turned bright red radiating to his lily white ears; even his shiny bald head turned red. We wished and hoped that his threats far exceeded the reality of our impending punishment.

"That's a city park," he exclaimed, "now scarred and disfigured at your hands!" We didn't see the grandiosity of his worldview; we only saw a field of dying weeds and a dead tree. Clyde was a member of the city council and would have to explain to the city fathers about our juvenile delinquent debauchery. How would it look having his grandson defacing our beautiful city? We were marked for life, but there was a certain accountability for our action. We worked even harder at the dairy trying to regain Grandpa's favor. Paul Bunyan jokes began to surface as we routinely shoveled cow shit from the milking stalls. Clyde got out his chainsaw and cut the tree in short enough pieces for us to carry. He didn't take away Victor's knife or hatchet. We promised that we would only cut down willows for our forts. Finally, our misdeed was absolved.

My father once worked for Clyde at the dairy. My dad was quite a bit older than Jay. Vic and I watched our dads work together rebuilding Clyde's antique dairy farm equipment, tractors and manure spreaders. There was always something that needed to be fixed; it was a big job keeping the farm equipment in working order. On occasion there were mechanical parts left over, cast into a five-gallon bucket and designated 'extra parts'. Our dads did spread a lot of manure, drinking Lucky Lager beer as they worked. I rarely saw my father drive a car, and only a few times when he was drinking. He never did own a car during his lifetime. He could drive every other kind of farm and industrial machinery. There was no way I was ever going to meet his expectations. I'm not even sure that he had any, but I marveled at his ability to take a John Deere tractor apart and put it together again while he drank beer, focused like a laser on his task at hand.

Jay owned a new shiny turquoise and white '58 Ford Fairlane station wagon that Alice drove. Jay drove a rusty faded green '53 International pickup truck, the box filled with scattered alfalfa hay and cow shit. Jay and Alice were quite young compared to my parents. Alice was half my mother's age, and I always thought Victor was so lucky to have parents that would live a long time. Jay respected my father's natural mechanical abilities. Even though my parents were older, they didn't seem to fit in with any people in Harlem. They told Great Depression stories to guilt us into hoeing the garden. "We had to have a green thumb or starve," they assertively espoused. "We spent hours listening to stories and watching the corn grow to knee high by the 4th of July," Jay would say. My father and Jay were friends, making our own brotherhood stronger. The two fat kids from the North Side, Victor and I came to rely on each other during the rebelliousness of our adolescent years.

Victor's biggest hero was Grandpa Dan, and he told me stories of his grandpa's greatest adventures. One spring afternoon Grandpa Dan and Jack, his aging deputy, stopped on their way to the Hutterite colony. They were on official sheriff business. A local farmer had accused one of the Hutterite boys of stealing chickens, a criminal offense in Blaine County. Those boys were rumored to be the best chicken thieves in the county. Victor and I rode with Grandpa Dan and Jack to the colony. The Hutterites talked funny and dressed in strange black clothing. As Dan concluded his search for the chicken thief, we heard him strike up a deal to trade Vic and me for a bottle of homemade wine. As he bartered with the Hutterite man, we blanketed ourselves in silence in the furthest corner of the trunk to avoid chicken thief slavery.

The North Harlem Colony was five miles north of town; the Hutterites were hard working people and grew the best garden vegetables. They were famous for their fresh eggs, and they all dressed in a common style. The women wore long polka-dot dresses with kerchief scarves on their heads. The men dressed in black pants with suspenders and colorful plaid shirts. They were of German descent and spoke with a German accent. Dora and Jake Hofer came to school in Harlem the next year. Jake was a bully – nobody liked him. He was rebellious and always challenged the teachers. Dora was easy going, although she was teased and humiliated by the Harlem girls with their juvenile viciousness. We got to be friends briefly, mostly because they were treated as badly as us half-breeds at Lincoln Elementary School.

Once school was out, Victor and I worked during the summer feeding the milk cows at Grandpa Clyde's dairy. They all stood with 'cow-eyed' expressions while Jay, Grandpa Clyde, my dad and Johnny Rodriguez tended the milking machines, separators and coolers. Victor and I carried buckets of oats and grain to feed the smelly beasts standing in the metal-framed stalls. The grain was stored in a homemade trailer that we crawled into to fill the buckets. It took most of the morning getting our short legs in and out of the trailer. When that was done we started shoveling cow shit to the end of the milk house and onto a huge pile just outside the door. For our hard day's work, we earned a shiny five cent pierce, a butterhorn pastry and a glass of fresh, cold dairy milk. We desperately tried to emulate our dads – they were our hero role-models. They always finished their day with a cold Lucky Lager beer.

Johnny Rodriguez was related to one of the migrant Mexican families who came to eastern Montana every year to harvest sugar beets. The sugar beet crops were a significant source of income to the local farmers. At the dairy Johnny helped Victor and me with the heavy lifting and shoveling of manure out the door to the huge pile below. Ironically, Victor and I had our most in-depth political conversations shoveling that huge pile of shit. That's where Victor learned the fine art of political oratory. He was a shoe-in during the class president election. Victor was in the 'smart white kid' classroom at school. We only saw each other at recess and lunch, where I was lined up in the special lunch line for poor kids. The humiliation came with everyone knowing you were on AFDC welfare. It was the only reality I had ever known. There was no escape from poverty for most poor people…there still isn't. If you try to get ahead, the government pushes you back into the dirt with determination to keep you in your place.

Alice was loading film into her camera as I approached their house. Victor's pony, Little Joe, was saddled and tethered to the wagon-wheel fence. Victor was already in the saddle. Jay thought it was a brilliant idea to take a photograph of Victor and his Lakota friend. Little Joe was Victor's very own pinto pony, just like the one on Bonanza. I stood on the hay bale, imitating Victor. Jay struggled to get me in the saddle behind my brother Vic for the photograph. I unwillingly agreed in spite of the shame my Lakota warrior ancestors must have felt, laughing and rolling in their Lakota graves. I am sure all must have seen the fear on my face as Alice took the picture. I'd had enough; it was time to get off before I fell off. I didn't care – I was not getting back on that pony again so my mother could see me riding behind Victor.

During the summer Johnny Rodriguez found time to teach Victor and me the 'dirty words' in his Mexican language. Paying close attention to every word, we sounded out the syllables like linguistics students. Victor and I practiced while Johnny was working. We learned what *pendejo* meant, and there were many at our school. We repeated after Johnny as he grinned at our progress. *Chingo de madre. Chingo de madre, pendejo. Besa me culo, pendejo.* Victor and I repeated our newly acquired international Mexican language to our white and Indian friends at school. They were so impressed with our expertise, they wanted to learn, too. We spent many recesses practicing assimilation and accommodation of our new linguistic skills, inserting liquid and crystalized intelligence into our long-term memories. When Johnny left, so did our access to this new world of words.

Slim Ragsdale was in a rare drinking mood. He and my father talked about those drunken 'wards of the government'.

Slim belched Lucky Lager breath telling my father, "Hell yeah, Johnny! I'm part Cherokee…I grew up in the Oklahoma Hills," he went on talking. With every beer he became more certain. Indian people need to pull themselves up by their bootstraps taking care of other peoples' ranches and driving government road graders. His internalized racism was blatantly consistent with his naivety. It wasn't uncommon; it was obvious he was ashamed of who he was. He wanted desperately to be white. His son Billy repeated his father's stories about the Oklahoma Hills, just like a country song. Billy learned to sing an Oklahoma yodel and play his magic Silvertone guitar. Years later after all the beatings Slim gave him, Billy in his late teens finally ran away to the Oklahoma Hills to get away from his father's lariat rope. Bet he found other kids there he could use to his benefit. That's just the way he was. I wouldn't be surprised if he is still doing it today.

Our second grade class at Lincoln Elementary was elated – it was finally Friday. The date was November 22, 1963. The morning had been consumed with reading about Dick and Jane, mathematic times tables and our *Weekly Readers*. It was just after noon recess when the news came; it spread quickly throughout the school. The teachers cried as the school bell rang. Adult tears flowed when the solemn announcement came that President Kennedy was shot. School dismissed for the day, which usually brought cheers from unwilling participants, but today there were none. The quiet came over Harlem, and even the cars and buses drove slowly in solace for the country's great loss. My mother was emotionally shaken, just like the rest of the country. His picture hung above the door in our five room mansion. She was a great admirer and disregarded rumors of his romance with Marilyn Monroe, although all the young boys were envious with imagined fantasies.

Social conditions were not much different in Harlem, Montana, then they were in the south. They had their 'niggers' and we were the 'redskins'. White people in Harlem thought nothing of discrimination, it was accepted and expected. The difference was that in the south white people killed niggers; in Montana redskins had killed their pioneer ancestors. Still, the country's treatment of blacks and Indians wasn't much different in 1963. The Birmingham bombing shook the country with hatred. The white supremacists simply justified their evil with their Christian religion and blue-eyed Jesus. My teacher asserted that negroes needed to know their place. We read in our *Weekly Reader* about the black devil, Malcolm X, who wanted to kill all the white people and the Lakota, too. Our teacher explained that if only they knew their place like the Indians, negroes could also live in peace. When I asked my mother, she said Malcolm X was a war chief who had a Ghost Dance vision and spoke for all poor people and that the white people were afraid of his truths.

In school I learned first-hand about authoritarian bureaucratic institutions, a real 'No Child Left Behind' lesson of *See Dick jump. See Spot run. Run, Lakota, run.* We were forced to recite the Pledge of Allegiance and told complete lies that our teachers learned in their history books. The story about the white man legend of the Pilgrims sharing Thanksgiving with the Indians was one of the first lies, told to distill the white man's guilt for his greed and hatred. White invaders slaughtered an estimated 60,000,000 native people across the Americas and now they question our trust? Victor and I fought our own Indian wars, side by side, with our hero John Wayne. Victor died many deaths for the white man shame. He always died like a good Indian. I never did own a pair of boots. It wasn't the Lakota-Chippewa way. My nephew, Jerry, went on a different road of institutionalization, and Billy Ragsdale soon drifted away when our friendship ended in 1965.

Chapter 14

Field of North Side Dreams

Montana winters dragged on past the spring solstice. When my father was home and I was bored, he taught me how to play chess. We played game after game, and I always lost. I never knew the formality; I learned by trial and error, losing every time. The many games were training for life's challenges. A pawn and a queen still have a chance and kings are worthless. Chess was the only real communication we had. Those games spoke millions of words and told thousands of stories. I surprised myself one day and won, but I always wondered if it was by accident or if he just didn't want to play anymore. Pinochle was our family communication. I was usually partners with Victor, but his hand signals never helped very much. His parents were no easier challenge than mine. The only difference was my mother no longer allowed beer in her house unlike Victor's house.

Victor and I, against all odds, were still best friends. We had been through thick and thin in our young adolescence. Even though I always bossed him around, he was the only person I could talk to about the important stuff. He watched Art Richman get the best of me at Grandpa Clyde's and witnessed how much I wanted to hate white people. I couldn't hate Victor, and I was more than half white. It was a dilemma we shared. Victor was Tantanka Íyotake and I was John Wayne. We walked up Highway 241 on our way to school. He told me that he was going to be moving to Livingston the next month. Jay had found a job there doing road construction. They were moving to Livingston to a house on H-Street. He would be starting school there in the fall. His dad was already there. His family was packing, and his mom had rented out their big pink house.

Coreen and Carl Robertson moved into Victor's house. Coreen was Laura Malley's daughter, and she had a sister named Donna. Donna wore a skimpy two-piece bathing suit in the summer. She was every young prepubescent boy's wet dream. Coreen and her husband were nice people; my mother and my sister knew them. We visited them, but the house wasn't the same without Victor's family. The big pink house missed Alice's yelling, mostly at Victor for not taking care of his sister. It missed Jay's dissociative coping skills, boisterous humor and belly laugh. Sometimes I wondered if Victor wasn't the parent – he always seemed to manage to maneuver through the minefield like a skilled politician in the halls of Congress. Chaos was normal at Victor's house. The effects of the genocide reeked at our house, carried by genetics and demonstrated through behavior.

The year passed slow as molasses, but it did finally pass, just like a bad case of gas. It was incredibly boring. Billy and I didn't hang out much anymore. We'd had a psychic parting of ways, disconnecting our trust. He hung out with the white supremacist south side cowboys from school. They were short on mentality and long on stupidity for the most part, true *pendejos*. There was nothing left in common.

I came home from an insignificant day of school and cognitive dissonance. With a toothless grin, my mom handed me a letter in Victor's handwriting…he was moving home as suddenly as he had left. Our reunion was uneventful, as if he had never been gone at all. We resumed our friendship; we were back to bickering and arguing like brothers do. Victor's interest in politics was evident. It wasn't long before he resumed his position among his peers. They weren't capable of keeping up with his inherent gift for debate and bullshit that he learned from his ancestral fathers.

It was 1963 in Indian Country. Everything of value and virtue had been taken from native people across the Lakota nations. On the Fort Belknap Reservation across the Milk River from Harlem, poverty and despair was a common experience for the White Clay and Nakoda people as well. Some of our Chippewa-Cree cousins were even poorer than our Lakota-Chippewa family. After all, we lived in a five room mansion with running water. My cousin Norman lived in a two room tan stucco house in the middle of the Harlem's west side with his four Nakoda-Chippewa sons. He searched for his 'bootstraps', but he never found them either. Norman hid his shame with gregarious humor, a well-defined defense mechanism. Norman's youngest son, Robert, found his way to my mother's sympathy. Robert always came home with me to share our feast of homemade bean soup and frybread that floated on air. Mom always sent extra home for his brothers – it was First Holy Woman's traditional Lakota ways.

I was never quite sure why my Nakoda-Chippewa cousins didn't like Victor. Maybe he was an easy target for them to bully. He was never much at fighting, he mostly talked until he got beat up or wore them down with his gift of gab. I assumed it was because he was white and different from the rest of us in my Lakota-Chippewa-White Clay-Nakoda mixed up breed family. Perhaps they were taking out their historical grief on him. Waynie always found a reason to pick a fight with Victor. It was my due diligence to protect my brother from my cousints wrath. I never hesitated to rescue Victor from the grips of their misguided anger. After all, I was usually the scapegoat for all the white privilege kids at school and knew how Victor felt. I was one of the *red shadow* people, a Lakota, and the shame of their ancestors' genocidal humanity.

There were no black people in Montana's Harlem except for old Jimmy Walls, and we always heard he was a Cherokee. All of his kids were half Indian. His wife, Edith, was Nakoda and from a respectable family. She raised her children in poverty, but with dignity. There was a lot of excitement in 1964. I didn't understand what it meant, but President Johnson gave the 'niggers' the right to vote. The white men in Harlem thought it was the worst thing that could ever have happened. For them, it was the worst 4th of July Harlem had ever seen. "Shit…them niggers can't even read! The next thing you know them porch monkey darkies will be givin' these fuckin' Indians ideas…then they'll want equal fuckin' rights, too!" You heard the same small talk where ever white men gathered to pass judgement and talk about 'niggers' and 'injuns'. While the black man prayed, the white man burned his Christian cross.

The tickets came in the mail with $40 in a letter from my brother Babe's wife, Joan. Babe and Byo were both stationed at the Fort Lewis U.S. Army base south of Seattle. My mother packed and repacked and made frybread for the 24-hour Burlington-Northern train ride to Seattle. My first encounter with a black man was the porter on the train. "Hello sir, how are you today?" he asked in a kindly voice. He took off his porter's hat, waving to me and my mother as we searched for our seats. I had never been called 'sir' before. Still in awe, I looked behind me finally replying, "Fine, thank you." We found our seats; when he came by to take our tickets, he played *Tom Dooley* on his Marine Band harmonica. I was amazed at how he made those harmonic sounds, the wailing that sounded like tears floating through the air. My mother let me move to a closer vacant seat to hear his melody with the rhythm of the wheels on the railroad tracks.

The ride was long and we watched the scenery and towns pass by. The railroad only goes by the poor peoples' houses, just like that log cabin shack we lived in before we moved into our five room mansion with running water. My curiosity was young and I wanted to learn about everything there was to know. I never trusted the books I was forced to keep in my desk at school; I trusted my own eyes…*for spacious skies, amber waves of grain…mountain majesties above the fruited plain.* The train slowed, it seemed forever, slowly passing the industry and poverty of the city, before grinding to a halt. The black porter called out our arrival in Seattle. Passengers gathered their belongings and patiently waited for their turn to exit the train car onto the depot platform. I had never seen so many people all in one place. They spoke in foreign languages and accents. Joan greeted us at the train depot. We found our way to her '60 Chevy Belair. We drove through the dark into the unknown to arrive at the Fort Lewis army barracks housing.

The next morning the sun seemed to come up in the west, and it shone brightly in my eyes. My Lakota directions were disoriented from the night and the long ride. I was up, wide awake and following the laughter to the kitchen. Joan and my mother sat at the kitchen table drinking Folgers coffee. They exchanged news and family gossip from back home at Fort Belknap. Joan and my mom were friends, and Violet and my mother had known each other for years. I went outside to explore the surroundings and gather my directions. Within minutes Babe and Joan's son, Marvin Junior, came from around the back of the house. It didn't take long to remember how spoiled he was. He was a junior narcissist and demanded that all of his friends call him 'General' as he pointed to the star on his PX replica of an officer's hat. I did my best to avoid him after he intentionally slammed my finger in the car door.

The white kids I met weren't very friendly; I wondered if they knew the kids in Harlem. They were mostly concerned that their toys were accounted for when my nephew and I left their houses. There weren't any Indian kids anywhere in sight other than my annoying nephew. There was a black kid down the street across the road. He mostly hung out by himself. He sat on his front porch a lot and read books. I wondered why he wanted to spend all of his time reading when he had to read all year in school. He was tall and wiry like his father, a captain in the U.S. Army. His name was Marcus Anthony Davis and he was from Alabama. He was 12 years old and already knew he was going to be a pilot when he was old enough. Marcus's grandfather had wanted to be a pilot in World War II. His father had been in the Korean War and was going to retire someday.

I joked about Marcus's initials and he laughed with the joke. He was fascinated with Indians and wondered whether we really lived in tee-pees and ate buffalo…and dogs. He said that his grandfather had told him that when he was young. He showed me books about the Seminole and the funny way they dressed. I told him the stories about Sitting Bull and Crazy Horse that I had heard a thousand times. When we played cowboys and Indians, he always insisted on being the Indian, and I always insisted on being John Wayne. Marvin was General Custer. The 4th of July was the highlight of my summer with fireworks like I had never seen, the bombs bursting in air with showers of colored explosions drifting back towards earth. Thousands of people surrounded me as I watched in awe. I was swept away with the crowd. Patriotism ran rampant; I felt it embrace the audience, and I could hear the Pledge of Allegiance throughout the collective unconscious of the observers.

It was a long month before school started in 1964. We asserted our industrious efforts to resolve our athletic inferiority. Long before his friend Kevin Costner ever built his 'Field of Dreams', Victor had a vision for the field of weeds adjacent to the big pink house where he lived. He was inspired by the fact that we had absolutely no athletic aptitude. Our skills were marginal at best. The south side kids wouldn't let us play on their white privileged team of Harlem's finest stars. We north siders were an embarrassment and an athletic shame in the Harlem community. Even though we sucked, we were filled with the north side spirit and the determination to realize the all-American dream. Perhaps it was beyond our ability, but the journey is greater than the destination. So, we commenced our work project in an act of blind faith under Victor's direction.

Victor's grandpa owned the four-acre lot overgrown with four-foot tall milkweed. Victor and I got permission from Grandpa Clyde to use the field to fulfill Victor's vision. One of the requirements was that we had to promise not to cut down any more of the city's dead trees. Clyde was a cagey old horse trader. Getting us to work for free, he made a deal with us. Billy, Victor and me pulled weeds for days, then weeks until the field was cleared. Jay and my dad helped us erect a crude backstop with two creosote-soaked railroad ties and chicken wire. When the field was cleared and we had our chicken wire backstop, we played 'work-up' into the evening hours until dusk. Wiley Hilderman came to join us. He was younger than us, but he was a north-sider. Billy's brother, Raymond Ragsdale, didn't show up; he wasn't interested in anything but horses.

Our games took longer than most as we were miserable at both pitching and hitting. Still, we were determined to play those south side kids and give them the imaginary thrashing of our north side fantasies. The summer wore on, and the south side kids frequented our north side Wrigley Field in a covert coup attempt to take over our primitive stadium. Before long, the gravel street was filled with parked south-siders cheering on the south side kids. I guess white kids just want what they don't have. Once we stopped showing up, the softball games fizzled out. It just wasn't fun anymore. This was my first awareness of the 'haves' and 'have nots'. Victor defined this phenomenon as north side spirit. We pursued our lifetime endeavors with north side spirit reverberating throughout our lives.

We had barely gotten rid of our cap-guns and toy plastic army men; already adolescence was becoming increasingly confusing with the cognitive discord brought on by the presence of the female species. A few random encounters in falling-down barns and by the head gates along 30 Mile Creek filled my adolescent thoughts. I didn't mind their fleeting nature as long as we were certain to meet again. Life was becoming more of a grey area as I approached the concrete operational, industrious post-latency developmental period in my young inferior Lakota existence. I also experienced my first encounter with death, fear of the darkness and the eternal abyss, and it was terrifying. I had just ventured into the existential search for the answer to our being when Boyd Birch had a heart attack and died. He was one of my protectors; he had been a big help to my mother during hard times when the cupboards were bare. Boyd was one of the 'many feet' I'd seen in that old log shack at the edge of Harlem. He randomly showed up with a freshly killed deer and a hundred-pound sack of spuds he bought for $1.75 at the spud house.

Boyd was Aunt Katie Birch's only son. Katie was older than my mother, and she came to our house with Boyd to drink Lipton tea with Mom and share reservation gossip. Boyd was part of our family; he hung out with my brothers and cousins. They shared late night adventures, returning with a freshly killed 'slow elk'. It was a young warrior game. They methodically butchered and quartered up the carcass, saving the tripe and marrow gut for the White Clay and Nakoda elders. Katie always got the best of the best of the kill, and the elders thought they had just been given the finest of French delicacies, cuisine fit for a king. I would wake up late at night to hear the hushed voices as I peeked around the corner. When my mother saw me she 'shushed' me back to bed. I woke the next morning to the sound of her cheerfully humming and to the smell of the best Floyd Frye 'slow elk' cooking. It was the best I ever had in all my memories of my warrior cousints.

It is a dark memory, driving to Dodson for the funeral of this man who had been like one of my big brothers. Boyd's wife, Charlotte, Boo Boo as we knew her, was Aunt Dora and Uncle Raymond's daughter, so of course they were there. Boo Boo held her infant son as she silently wept. It was my first 'close up' experience with death, and it shook me to the core. I wondered what it was like to die, and where did we go after we died? I couldn't imagine that I would go anywhere but the Lakota hell to which I was born. I listened to the priest talk about Boyd's 'salvation', but I knew Boyd had already gone to the Creator with his grandfathers, Chief Nosey and The Boy. There was an empty hole in our lives when he passed. He wasn't very old, quite young, actually. Death was around the corner, a short instant, life vanishing from our neuro-synaptic illusion of an imagined world – into the world beyond this one, the spirit of all things. That is the real world behind this one, and everything we see here is something like a shadow from that world. Boyd was on his horse in that world, and the horse and himself on it and the trees and the grass and the stones and everything were made of spirit, and nothing was hard, and everything seemed to float. It took a while to accept that death was imminent. Someday my mother and father were going to die. All the people in their lives had died. Someday it would be my turn, and it was a terrifying thought. I dreamed again about the white buffalo, Big Medicine, and saw him vividly standing in the morning frost. We all have to die alone, like Boyd, a journey he had to take. If the Christian Jesus died for his sins, he was forgiven for hanging out with my cow thieving family. Creator gave him honor for his coup on Floyd Frey. The emotional discord subsided, life returned to normal. Victor and I talked about our fears and the legacies we would leave someday. He was expected to do great things; there weren't any expectations for me. I couldn't even think of any. I had never heard of any expectations for any Indian other than Tonto, and that was on TV.

It was the beginning of Victor's and my musical futures and the realization of our north side determination. Victor ordered the advertisement for guitar lessons in the Carlton Comic book, *'Be popular in only 7 days!'*. He got a cheap Sears and Roebuck $9 guitar for his birthday. It was stained mahogany brown and had a wagon train painted on the front. It was a fine guitar; Gene Autry and Cowboy Copas would have been proud to use it on any Grand Ol' Opry Saturday night. Victor had been inspired by my brothers, Babe and Byo. He listened intently to Babe's tales about how he was only 15 years old when he went to fight the U.S. Government's war. It was just another war against the 'Indians' in a faraway Asian country called Korea. I told Victor about my mother's version of the tears she wept while waiting for the U.S. Government car to come to the front door and how she envisioned the empty blank stare of the man who would tell her she had lost her eldest son fighting those 'dirty savages'.

After the Korean War my brother Babe spent several years drinking and driving around Germany in a Volkswagen bus. His job in the U.S. Army was playing honky-tonk hillbilly music entertaining the troops and filling his unhealthy Lakota-White Clay alcohol addiction. Babe was still angry with his father; every drink he took was a blow to his White Clay legacy and a determination to be white. He left his Lodge Pole family behind – we weren't good enough for his new assimilation to the white world. He easily transitioned to the white ways. Victor and I sat quietly listening as my brothers and their friends grew louder. The tales grew wilder with every song they sang and every Lucky Lager beer they drank in their resolve to get to the bar before the fight began. I was sure the 'dirty scrap' waited for them. It always did, just like whiskey drenched clockwork.

I could tell from the look on his face, Victor was calculating and analyzing the possibilities of learning the guitar in only seven days. We could be stars. Victor's wagon train guitar brought him imaginary fame on the Dick Cavett Show, right after Pat Boone and Ricky Nelson. Made for stardom, he arranged for lessons with Jay Glenn, a local singing buckaroo who was already in high school. Victor diligently took lessons and learned how to play a 'G' chord with two fingers, then he progressed to the 'C' chord. The one that finally stumped Victor was that dog-gone 'F' chord; his short stubby fingers just couldn't hold down the strings. The drums became his new aspiration. He had rhythm in his soul and the determination to be the hit of the party. His enthusiasm was infectious and was seldom questioned. I was the skeptic that held him to the ground.

My sister-in-law's dad came from California driving a '62 Chevy Corvair convertible. It was shiny blue with a white ragtop that had a few holes. Fortunately, it hardly rained in eastern Montana in the summers. Bill Shields was in his mid to late fifties. He was a full blood Assiniboine man, and as impressionable as we were at 12 years, we hung on every word listening to tales of his life in the big cities of Los Angeles and Hollywood. He told us about Native American spirituality and his experiences in the white man world. That was his reason for coming home; he couldn't understand the way they lived. It was the Relocation Era, the years when the U.S. Government sent Indians to the city to survive or perish. Victor's and my eyes grew wide seeing the pouch of neatly rolled pegi'. Bill told us how pegi' had been used for ceremony by our ancestors before there were hippies in San Francisco. "Aw shore cudn't wait ta get home, aw toll dose fellas at dat Relacashun Office, so aw came soon as aw cud, n'it!" he said. He handed Victor and me the neatly rolled pegi' he'd lit seconds before. The ash smoldered, burning my finger as my brother Marvin pulled into the driveway. I was still stunned. It would take time to accommodate this information into my new world view. We weren't unique in our rebellion; it was our genetics! It confirmed what Aunt Sis had shown me.

I inherited the wagon train guitar after Victor decided he was going to be a drummer just like his cousin, Buddy Rich. Buddy was a distant relative to Victor's Grandma Rich, who lived way out on the west coast in Oregon, "Ya know, by golly." We watched the Dick Cavett show every time Buddy Rich was on. He was a jazz drummer and one of the best, I was told. Black people weren't allowed to have their own shows, so it was debatable. Only white musicians were afforded the luxury of nation-wide television and production exposure. Pat Boone stole perfectly good black songs with no credit given to the original artists. He took *Tutti Fruiti* as a follow up to *Love Letters in the Sand*. None of these facts slowed Victor down. He fashioned his first set of drums from assorted Folgers and MJB coffee cans held together with black plastic electrical tape. It took a few years before Victor had a 'real' set of plastic-tipped drum sticks. In the meantime he used No. 2 pencils, rulers, wooden dowels and any other object he could fashion into a Lakota war club.

Since we didn't have a TV, I went to every movie that came to the Grand Theater. The Clint Eastwood spaghetti westerns were very popular. Clint was the new idol of high testosterone rednecks. John Wayne was aging with True Grit; he was nearing the end of his era of hero worship, like Hop-along Cassidy and the rest. Victor had to babysit his younger sisters, so I hung out with Charley and his friend, Garth. I knew him from school, he played drums. We were at the old Rambler Garage, smoking the little bit of homegrown pegi' we had. We seriously inhaled the chlorophyll in anticipation of a groovy cinematic experience. Garth had learned to roll, and he showed his finest skills. As we came around the corner, Lee Parks drove up in his '68 Cougar. He said he'd just gotten some 'acid' from his older brother, Allen, and wanted to sell us some. It was 25 cents a hit and Lee said it took two to get off. I bought four and took them all. Garth bought two and took one; Charley bought two and expanded his universe. We continued on to the Grand Theater where the new release, *Barbarella*, was playing.

We got our Coke and popcorn and headed into the theater. As we searched for our seats, my steps pounded in my ears like a bass drum. My focus faded in and out in psychedelic swirls of awareness. The air sparkled with ice crystals, and our voices reverberated in faint frozen echoes. We settled into the worn seats and my body started to tingle as the lights went dim. I looked to the right…the left side of Garth's face was melting. When he laughed, the sound danced from his mouth in a rainbow of color. When he spoke, the words came out as psychedelic letters. I turned forward to watch the cartoon. Mr. Magoo and I shared our liquid concept of reality. As *Barbarella* began, I let my adolescent fantasy of Jane Fonda play in my head. I hadn't a clue what the movie was about. The faces melted in the darkness of the theater.

It was an enlightening experience I shared with a White Clay cousin. My attachment was more than childish innocence. The emotional exploration created confusion about the whole complicated concept. I finally understood my parents' relationship. My confused formal operational identity was shamefully aware that my mother and father were first cousins. It was a shocking experience, and I felt that I embodied the entirety of the 'family shame'. I searched for hints, but I never felt the shame from my mother. My father, on the other hand, was a different story; I felt my existence in this world was his genital shame. I only saw him cry once as I walked by mom's door, he was alone, sitting on the bed with his head hanging down sobbing softly. It was obviously my fault. I screamed from my cellular being, trying in desperation to speak to him…he still never heard me.

Chapter 15

If Teardrops Were Pennies

Victor and I listened to his red and white RCA Victor phonograph, spinning Sandy Dennis records endlessly. We made plans for musical fame. Weeks and months passed, and I learned guitar chords from my older brother and sister. I practiced diligently playing the wagon train guitar in the outhouse. I thought I was out of hearing range, but my father overheard me and joked with sarcastic criticisms. I practiced Hank William's song, *I'm So Lonesome I Could Cry*, and the minor chord made a dark, lonely Lakota sound. I thought about blue curtains blowing in a gentle summer breeze, the ancient carnal voices that rejected the white world. I listened even though I didn't understand the words. Victor and I never considered the fact that we were marginal on talent. Never letting that stop us, we embarked on our Ghost Dance journey. Victor's cousin Charlie Hay wasn't really interested in joining our band, but Vic convinced him we would be stars. We could learn to play like those English bands in the movies.

Victor got invited to the white junior high 'private by invitation only' parties. I kept practicing, experimenting with different sounds on my single pick-up Sears and Roebuck guitar. The east side was where all the rich Harlem kids lived, the Olsons, Fuzesys, Orlandos and of course the Rasmussens. Victor was born to be the hit of the party. He got invited to every event during our 7th and 8th grade years. I tried not to let on that it bothered me; I didn't want Victor to know. It might have been an admission that I wanted their acceptance. I wanted to get away from them and the feeling of inferiority and shame I felt just being around them. There was no way out of my poverty – no bootstraps to pull up. Unless you were blond with blue eyes, there wasn't much opportunity. It was remarkable how differently people with brown eyes were treated in the big flat country of Scandinavian Blaine County. For some reason, Victor eventually decided, "Those parties are never any fun." He never mentioned it again, but he stopped going to their exclusive parties.

As our social sophistication developed, our drinking skills more refined, Victor became the hit of Harlem's 'Rock' parties. We discovered Motown and he discovered his soul moves. Victor's cousin Charlie and I tried smoking some banana peels. All we got was a big fat Yellow Submarine headache. We experimented with the multiple effects of alcohol, pegi' and psychedelic Crazy Horse visions. We drove around in Gary Parnell's Chevy Impala drinking F.I. Muscatel wine with Goofy Wing sometimes called Crooked Shank and Eggfart Allen, listening to the Four Tops and the Temptations. Eggfart was my second or third cousin, however you wanted to count it. He was full of shit like most of my relatives, with a twisted and warped sense of humor. We focused on the traditions passed down from our uncles, laughing and joking about the corruption of their minds with alcohol, the honorary tribal member. Gary was getting back to his Gros Ventre roots. He was in rebellion against the establishment and his middle class parents.

Even in Harlem we were aware of the civil rights movement and the struggles of black people. My mother grieved when Malcolm X was murdered, and she prayed for his family. I remember listening to the news on KOJM 6.10 radio. It was 1969 and the struggle for equality continued, even as the country lamented Martin Luther King's death just months before. Although there wasn't a black community in Harlem, it again came to my preconscious mind that there was a lot of racism to go around. This awareness gave identity to the feeling I felt in my 15-year-old gut every time I encountered Ronny Orlando, Allen Fuzesy, Art Richman or the other asshole pricks that assumed white privileged superiority. I found it hard to believe that I had ever wanted to be friends with these people. There was only so many insults on my lineage, my race and my size to be tolerated. I kneed Ronny in the balls during the heat of battle. He was a year and a half older than me, but his dad screamed at me that I dang near ruined the family jewels. Then he grabbed me by the front of my coat, lifting me off the ground in a white supremacist rage.

Victor and I diligently pursued our musical career, becoming more sophisticated as time went by. Victor earned money selling his wool and lambs at the Blaine County Fair. He saved assiduously in a separate fund until he had enough to purchase a set of drums. We searched out Roddy Shawl, the drummer for the famous *Ray Doney and the Tumwater Boys*. We heard he had his drums for sale. Ray was friends with my brothers, Babe and Byo, and he was always at our house for jam sessions and Lucky Lager beer when my brothers were home on furlough. The drum set had possibly been new at one time back in the 1920's. It had a dilapidated 28-inch bass drum with a 12-inch mounted tom-tom. The floor tom-tom was a converted 14-inch marching snare. There were two broken Japanese symbols and no cymbal stand.

Victor counted out $32.50 and a star was born. It was a deadly but ingenious idea – since Victor had no cymbal stands, we hung the two broken cymbals from the ceiling with baling twine in the broken-down bunkhouse where Johnny Rodriguez lived on Grampa Clyde's dairy. We looked at rare Carvin bass catalogues in the comic book advertisements. I found a Hagstrom guitar catalogue from which Charlie dreamed of having such quality instruments. Victor stole old music catalogues from the high school band room. He borrowed his favorite Zildjian cymbal which he forgot to return for the next 50 years. It would eventually become one of the amends he made in his AA resolutions. The baling twine was a great idea until Victor went into one of his Buddy Rich drum solos and the cymbals swung erratically out of control. They circled the room slicing the air, each with deadly aim. By the time Victor reached the crescendo, Charlie and I had to duck to survive Victor's misguided cymbal crashes. The lethal discs severed the atmosphere in our 14-foot by 13.7-foot chamber of creative expression.

Wally, Richard and Danny were Victor's and my classmates in elementary and junior high school. They were miniature white boys. All the girls swooned over their Nehru jackets, paisley shirts and corduroy pants with wide leather belts. The aesthetic value of the dingo boots was more than the girls could take. Wally's father, Clifford Mummey, drove the road grader. He considered himself important as the 'city engineer' of Harlem. There really wasn't much to do other than grade the roads and make sure the water was drinkable. Clifford passed by our house driving the road grader north, moving the winter's hard pan to the center of the road. Then he turned around at the city limits, just past Wilson's house, and slowly drove south. Wally's mother, Gladys, worked at the New England Bar for her sister-in-law, Ida, who was married to Clifford's brother, Lloyd. At the New England, it was usually a long wait for my father to finish his Lucky Lager beer and his shots of Seagram's 7. Ida or Gladys would feel sorry for me and give me an ice cold Orange Crush soda pop. Sometimes I got a bag of salty potato chips that went perfectly with the pop. Life was good then.

Richard's father, Bill Mohar, was from a Big Flat farming family and was certainly akin to white privilege. Bill's wife was Mrs. Fitzimmon's daughter, Annie. Mrs. Fitzimmon and my mother were friends, maybe related somehow, although I wasn't quite sure. I think somewhere back in the 1920's or '30s a couple of cousins were married, profoundly joining two huge families, with all the cousins, of course. Mrs. Fitzimmon and my mother chatted like two meadowlarks in their soft-spoken Indian voices when passing on the street. She was a few years older than my mom. Richard never let on that he was part Indian and I certainly never knew which part. He tried to hide his ancestral shame as he asserted his white paternal right. Richards mother and father drank like two Lakotas after a Big Flat drought. Annie had an infectious laugh that could be heard throughout the VFW Club. Richard was short for his age. He walked on his tip toes to see the white privileged sky. Richard viewed himself as the star of the Harlem Wildcats basketball team and himself as ten feet tall.

Richard was only an Indian when he went to Indian Health Services for free U.S. government medical care. I went to his house a few times where he asserted his superiority, making sure we were never very close. I could take or leave his superficial friendship, learning that some friendships were a convenience to be exploited. Withdrawing was a common defense mechanism, and I just stopped talking to him when he found the white world. It was a place no Lakota-Chippewa prairie-nigger would ever be welcomed. No matter how 'white' you thought, you were still a fucking prairie-nigger. I think I hated me more than they did. Victor, on the other hand, naively bought into the white supremacy briefly; he moved back and forth between the two innocuous worlds. He wore a Ghost Dance shirt in a world of Crazy Horse visions.

Danny's father, Dan O'Leary, was the postmaster at the U.S. Postal Service in Harlem. He was a quiet gentle man, he never seemed to get upset, the 'father knows best' sort of personality. He didn't drink alcohol at the bars like most of the parents I knew. He went to work, went home and lived his life quietly from the rest of the Harlem dysfunction. His father, Steve, owned the O'Leary Chevron station downtown. Danny's grandfather Steve was sympathetic to Indian kids and didn't share the implicit hate that I felt from most white people. Danny's mother, Mary, was a nurse at the Fort Belknap Indian Health Service hospital. She tried to calm me when I ran my hand through the old washing machine wringer when I was four years old. I always appreciated her kindness as it was rare in a white Montana town. It must have rubbed off on Danny because he spoke softly like his father, you might even say he was a little bit shy. Susan was the youngest and Mary Ann was his older sister. They all shared the similar demeanor of their parents.

Danny got a new Teisco guitar for Christmas. It was a triple pick-up with a vibrato whammy bar. Pretty high class by Victor's and my low standards. I went to practice Creedence Clearwater Revival's *Lodi*. "Just about a year ago…I set out on a road…seeking my fame and fortune…looking for a pot of Lakota gold," but there wasn't any to be found on the north side of the tracks in our five room mansion with running water. So where was our road to the middle class? Who was going to uplift us from poverty? I usually tried not to let my friends know it mattered, but I shared it with them in my early stages of drinking Lucky Lager and Seagram's 7. Victor and Danny were in Cub Scouts together in grade school; we had all known each other since first grade. The inspiration for stardom was an obsession for us. Victor, Danny and I conspired to start a rock and roll band. Before long, Richard and Wally joined, along with their Nehru shirts. There was a musical coup. Victor came to me, only because he was my best friend. He gave me the news – I was kicked out of the band.

I went back to the outhouse to learn more songs...*Louie, Louie...*'C', 'F', 'Gm'...and...*Gloria...*'E', 'D', 'A'. I only fell for the trick a couple times, always asking me back to the band to teach them new songs then kick me out once they learn the notes. They asked me to join the band one last time, so I taught them the wrong notes I learned. Victor always regretted the betrayal, the first in our long 11-year friendship. I never let him forget it; we joked about it every time I wanted to manipulate his white man guilt. Wally and Danny gave it their best. They had the rock star look, but were a little short on determination. That confounded 'F' chord ended a lot of rock and roll dreams; it was a passing phase for such aspirations. Dribbling a basketball was much easier. They excelled in their own right. Besides, the Spinet church organ wasn't easy to move on the toboggan. Victor and I regrouped, heading back to Grandpa Clyde's north side bunkhouse for another year of practice.

The 'Pit' was the old basketball court for the elementary grades in Lincoln Grade School. The junior high classrooms were in the new addition to the building. The Pit was where legions of poor dumb white and Indian predecessors were sent to display their shame, failure and anger. They were cursed with being poor or worse...Indian...worse yet...poor Lakota-Chippewa. I was able to avoid the sentence of shame for the most part. I learned to play a good dumb Indian. If you demonstrate no ability, there are no expectations and most white people leave you alone to your failure. The teachers are paid to be nice, so they don't really count. Mr. Dixon tried to manhandle Frogbreath and he got put against the wall. Frogbreath was 16 and drove his car to school in 8th grade. Mike Green was from Detroit and exuded an excessive city persona for Harlem. The junior high dance was going strong in the Pit when Victor and I went with Frogbreath to drink and drown our

Lakota dreams. We manifested the idiopathic sophistication of our fathers' loss of ego function.

The junior high dances were for white kids. They learned to socialize, rehearsing the formal operational mating rituals inherent in the confused identity of the Freudian genital stage. This was elementary crap for a young Lakota who was intent on his own alcoholic self-destruction. The 'sock hop' filled the room with the tinny sound of the phonograph blasting, "I'm so dizzy…my head is spinning" on a scratched 45 rpm vinyl record. The farm boys lined up on one side of the Pit; the farm girls lined up on the other side. The Indians lined up in the 'pisser' to drink Seagram's 7. We had to get primed for the case of Lucky Lager beer stashed in the weeds across the tracks. I had until 1:00 am to sneak back into the house without being caught. Unfortunately, while sleeping that night, the respired alcohol odor was a dead giveaway. My mother kept my secret even though I didn't want her to know. I thought it would upset her, as I always challenged her every effort to keep me out of trouble. Mamma tried.

No self-respecting south sider dared venture to the north side of the tracks. Our beer was safe behind the grain elevator by Henry Miller's place. Henry taught hunter safety classes. I went to the NRA gun safety class a couple times with Billy. I didn't have a gun, so I guess I didn't really learn anything useful. Henry's wife worked at the IHS hospital. She had been a World War II nurse and had her own traumatic memories. She spent three years in the European theatre. My Azure cousins and John Short were skilled in the fine art of drinking our stashed Lucky Lager beer. That was the rumor in school anyway. If there was a gang in Harlem, I guess they were the closest thing we had. I wasn't included in their circle. They never trusted me, I guess because Victor and I were friends. There was no denying he was white, but it didn't matter to me; he was my brother.

Billy learned to play guitar from Jay Glenn. He got pretty good with his Chet Atkins style of finger picking. He had a natural gift, but attention deficit hyperactivity disorder interrupted his focus. He never played a song all the way through – he fantasized beyond his own reach. Billy owned the only guitar amplifier on the north side. He let us use it to rehearse for our first big concert show. Victor announced to Charley and me there was an upcoming talent show. He entered the contest in spite of my insistent protests, begging him not to embarrass us. Victor was never one to avoid embarrassment to occupy a stage. Charley, Victor and I practiced endlessly, building neural pathways of Grand Canyon proportions. All we knew were four chords, but we practiced them to perfection…over and over…'A', 'G', and 'F major', then at last, the magic 'E' chord. It was summer and Harlem was short on quality entertainment.

With the coming stress of our fist rock and roll show, we practiced until our fingers were raw and bloody. The droning sound played in my head long after we put the guitars down for the day. In complete musical exhaustion, at last we were satisfied with our progress. As the date of the contest approached, I was more assertive than usual, making sure we had those four chords down to an infinite tee. In anticipation of our debut performance, Charley, Victor and I arrived at least eight hours early to the high school the day of the show. The music teacher helped us tune our Teisco guitars, giving us encouragement after seeing the stage fright in my eyes. Mr. Hanson asked Victor the name of our band. We looked at each other with blank stares…we hadn't thought of that yet. "I guess you are Victor and the Commons," Mr. Hanson said with a grin, giving reassurance of our success. We were going to be stars; fortune and fame was surely coming our poverty stricken way.

It was show time – the first contestant was Linda Hawley. She hesitantly walked on stage, standing shy and alone in front of the microphone. I knew I was in love when I heard her start to sing, "If teardrops were pennies and heartaches were gold…I'd have all the riches my pockets could hold." Her voice was the sound of an angel whispering. It sent shivers up and down my spine. I admired her yellow summer cotton dress, the matching bow in her long blond hair. Her father was Cranston Hawley. He used to cut meat at the Merry Market butcher shop when I was a kid, and his voice thundered like the voice of god. I knew there and then she was way too good for a Lakota from the northern-most side of the tracks.

The next act was announced, "Ladies and gentlemen…please give a big Harlem welcome to Franny and the Wagonmasters!" Francis Griffin played with Charley Pride; it was his claim to fame. They got drunk together in Helena with my sister, Annette. She bragged about it for years. Charley was quite a singer, but according to Francis, he taught Charley Pride everything he knew. Francis was a man of small stature, and he wore a black sequined shirt with a white bandana. He played an ES 335 Gibson Sunburst guitar. The Wagonmasters looked out of place, dressed in matching red cowboy shirts, cowboy boots and silk bandanas. These were the great grandsons of the infamous Charley Perry, the man who shot my grandfather, Mr. Allen. Charlie, Victor and I cringed as Franny strummed and sang *Your Cheatin' Heart*, the tearjerker song at the bottom of every bottle of Seagram's 7. Hank Williams must have been Lakota to sing a song so sad it makes your tears weep. It made me want to go to the outhouse and take a shit. The crowd cheered and stood to their feet as the curtain closed.

Charlie, Victor and I looked at each other and gulped. They had real Fender Bandmaster amps, equipment of which we only dreamed…and real guitars that played the right chords. We plugged in Billy's 30-watt Airline amplifier, Victor set his 28-inch bass drum in the center of the stage, and Charlie and I plugged in our Sears and Roebuck Teisco guitars. As the curtain opened

Victor counted, "One, two, three, four..." and we started the song just as we had rehearsed it, over and over. Somewhere during the performance, we knew we were dying in our shoes. Victor went into a bunkhouse solo that would have made Johnny Rodriguez proud. He channeled Buddy Rich, Sandy Dennis and Doug Clifford as the curtain closed. We heard the applause and cheers for Victor; his jazz inspiration saved the performance. It wasn't long before Victor and I were planning our first album and a concert tour all over Blaine and Phillips Counties.

Fred Thackery was the school bus driver in Dodson. We heard he let the Malta band use the bus garage for school dances. Victor got his phone number from the school and called him in hopes of a gig. It was fall, a good reason for a dance. All the farmers were done harvesting, everyone was back in school and the Dodson Fair was over. Dodson was a mix of white and Indian people, and most of the white people there were part Indian or had Indian friends – the kind they invited to their house, not just talked about to their white friends. Hell, some of my best friends are white, and some of them aren't too bad, even with their blue eyes and blond hair. Thackery's garage gave us a chance to express our creative genius, to find the perfect feedback and get our groove. We set up the amplifiers right after we swept the bus garage. That was all Fred asked of us was to leave it as we found it. There were assorted whiskey bottles and a few empty beer bottles left behind, nothing to cause any alarm.

In that same year, Charlie, Vic and I had our first grown-up encounter with Lucky Lager beer and the confabulated mutterings from the bottom of a whiskey bottle. We paid my cousin Sonny to buy a case of beer. We stashed it at our practice place along the bank of 30 Mile Creek. We started with a couple during our rehearsal break. It took hours to learn *The House of the Rising Sun*. It was an implication that the key to 'A minor' had unlimited possibilities. We finished the first six pack, then the next. By the time we finished the second, we were filled with youthful arrogance. We bravely staggered to Victor's house. Bouncing through the door, we arrived with shiny foreheads, proudly flaunting our remaining two six packs around the room. Charlie offered Victor's parents a beer. He offered one to Pete and Edna, too. The Siemens lived down the block, family friends of Jay and Alice. My dad worked for both of them at one time or another.

Jay and Pete played along with our novel presentation. Jay brought out a shiny virgin bottle of R&R Canadian whiskey. He proceeded to pass the fifth around in clockwise circles. Pete…then Charlie…now Jay…then Victor…and it was my turn. I played the three chords on the wagon train guitar while Jay and Pete sang out of whiskey tune, "There's a love-knot in my lariat…and it's waitin' for a blue-eyed prairie pet…while I'm ridin' the range all day…my lasso seems to say…it winds around an ornery stray…" Wilf Carter, was my mother's secret fantasy from the Lodge Pole fire of 1936. I wanted to show them our proud Lakota-Chippewa tradition. I took the remaining three swallows out of the bottle. Uncle Jay later tried to explain to my mother that he was trying to teach me a lesson, a lesson I was destined to repeat many times in my stubborn Lakota-Chippewa tradition.

Chapter 16

30 Degrees Celestial Longitude ($0° \leq \lambda < 30°$)

'The Castle' was restricted to only the most elite degenerates. They were all older than me by several years. I was allowed to enter because I was a friend of Rick Wilson. It was across the street from the Lincoln Grade School; I remember Jimmy and Edith Walls had lived there when I was in first grade. Rick and I both grew up on the north side of Harlem. Perhaps it was that north side poverty that kept us friends. I was still an outcast at school, but I didn't mind much anymore. Mostly I stuck to myself, avoiding Victor and Charlie's white friends. I was what most people might consider a loner. I am sure there are many reasons why people choose to be loners, but it all boils down to being alone. Roger Mummey was the 'Keeper of the Castle' and I was only allowed entry with Rick. The rooms were painted random colors – purple, green and orange. There were long beaded curtains separating the rooms.

I sat sipping a Lucky Lager beer trying to be invisible while Rick, Roger and Irv Booth mentally jousted with Terry Harris.

They separated the colored armies for a game of RISK. I'd never played the game before. Roger tried to explain it to me and handed me a piece of clear plastic acetate, "You'll figure it out," he said. Rick handed me the bottle of R&R whiskey. I put the piece of acetate on my tongue and washed it down with R&R. Roger put an eight-hour tape of psychedelic Blues Magoos, Strawberry Alarm Clock, Steppenwolf and Frank Zappa on his reel-to-reel tape deck. I tried to remain invisible as the LSD assumed its presence in my psyche. Irv and Roger continued their psychedelic banter, playing the 'mind fuck' games common to the Harlem counter culture.

The voices melted to indistinguishable thoughts. Rick and Roger debated over the color of their RISK armies and who was first to roll the dice. The sounds of voices swirled about the room in hues of reds, greens and blues with shades of deep purple, orange and yellow. Irv's face melted like a M.C. Escher painting. His feigned satanic laughter sent shivers down my back. Irv was the intellectual of the bunch. He talked about Plato and Socrates, the wise men of the ages. Rick and Roger made lewd comments about Kant. It crossed my mind whether the Lakota wise men had written books. As far as I knew, none of them knew how to read and they had no written language. The sun was coming up as the RISK game concluded. In spite of the Civil War in the United States, World War I, World War II, Korea and Viet Nam…it was obvious that the world was going to end in the Middle East, just like every game we played. The North Yemen Civil War and the Jordan-Palestine Civil War were obvious evidence in my delusional LSD thoughts. "Where in the hell did that come from?" I asked myself as the hallucinatory effects subsided.

Drugs and alcohol were our primary fascinations. School was the last thing on my mind. School was for stupid people; I knew better about that crap. The forced introjects were a dynamic in Gestalt Theory both the Pledge of Allegiance and the U.S.

Constitution weren't worth the hemp paper they were written on. I knew my place; I was the stereotype expectation. Bill Ragsdale's brother-in-law, John Morris, was the superintendent of Harlem High School. Bill's sister Peggy had married him several years before...out of the blue. It was obvious he didn't like Indians, but most people in Harlem didn't, so it wasn't anything unusual. The Viet Nam War escalated, as did conscientious objection to life in Harlem.

Back at school, out of boredom, 'The Herbie Freeman Press' emerged from a wild lysergic imagination. Gary Parnell shared with me his vision of Herbie Freeman who lived in his attic. Herbie was a metaphor that symbolized a revolutionary social conscience. I co-opted Gary's symbol of righteous resistance and built a coalition that included Victor, Brian Rowe and Tom Gould. Brian and Tom were Victor's nerdy white friends who got nothing but shit from the jocks and jokers. We printed our rebellious socialistic short-minded thoughts and beliefs that enraged John Morris, the authoritarian in our institutional bureaucracy. It was our right to free speech, regardless of our idiocies and immature idiopathic ideologies. I used every free minute, cranking the Harlem High School mimeograph machine; page after page I printed until the ink ran dry. Mr. Morris allowed free expression, but we had to buy our own ink and paper. Bill's mom gave us paper from the Harlem News where she worked. Victor used his 'wool money' to purchase ink supplies. This newspaper also presented an opportunity for an advertising assault promoting our new band named 'Logna'. Impropriety we stole the name from Bill Baker's band. Victor insisted we had to purchase our ad space to support the paper.

I was sleeping off the Lucky Lager dreams in algebra class when the door was thrown open. The principal looked like his eyes were about to pop out of his head, his face turning shades of purple to red. He boomed, "Conway!" waking the dreamer. "Come to the office," he managed, trying to hold back his rage.

I entered the principal's office, first seeing Brian and Tom sitting with sullen fearful faces. Victor and Bill were across the room at the other end of the bench. Victor read aloud from the newest edition of the Herbie Freeman Press, vocally blasting an article Brian had written. It highlighted American pragmatists opposed to escalating the U.S. role in Viet Nam, believing the economic cost of war too high. I dissociated as Mr. Morris began his raging rant, "Victor, you have potential…what are you doing still hanging around with these losers?" He pointed towards Bill and me. "I thought you knew better…I am so disappointed in you!" He turned to Brian and Tom, sunken into the wooden chairs, looking as if they wanted to piss their pants. "Brian…Tom…how in the hell did you guys get hooked up with these guys?" The rant continued to its crescendo. They shrank further into the wooden chairs as he stomped, then waved the most recent edition in the air.

"What the hell does this mean? L-o-g-n-a…the best F---ing band ever?" He growled trying to contain his rage. Victor came to the rescue, "It could mean 'fooling'," he offered. Tom chimed in, "It could mean 'farming' or 'funning'." Mr. Morris became even more enraged by these lame diversions, "You know damn well what it means…it means FUCKING!!!...how fucking stupid do you think I am?!" he shouted and stammered. "And you, Brian. Of all MY students, you should know better…now get the fu…hell out of my office!!!"

There was no pleasing him. All Indians were stupid to white people like him. There was no changing his mind. The school received funding as a result of the Johnson-O'Malley Act of 1934, reauthorized to provide public education services for Native Americans, poor dumb Indians like me. The only time white institutions have ever counted Indians is when they are asking for money from the government. Then we are counted in a census for a bureaucratic needs assessment. It's no different than when the Circle C Ranch regularly rustled government cattle on the hoof. Government actions designed to help the Indian, but end up benefitting only the white majority.

When we weren't in school, we were having way too much fun at the Rambler Garage. Once we pulled our vehicles inside, the police weren't able to come on the property without a search warrant. We drank a lot of Lucky Lager, the new shipment of pegi came to Havre and Tab got fresh LSD directly from San Francisco. Our friend, Bill Walls, experimented with the pegi' tradition. He was a jock, dead set against the medicine. He watched *Reefer Madness* and worried that he would jump off a skyscraper like Art Linkletter's daughter. He was pretty safe on that count since there were no skyscrapers in Harlem. I guess the old bank might do it if you were determined, but for the most part there were a few two-story buildings on Main Street and that was about the size of it. Times were changing fast in Harlem, and we weren't much interested in just drinking anymore. Don't get me wrong, it was still our mainstay, but there were other distractions.

Edith Walls and my mom were summoned to the school on an emergency. It couldn't wait, and they couldn't hesitate. Edith lived just four doors down the street from the Rambler Garage. The superintendent alleged that we Indians were up to no good smoking our indigenous medicine under their indigenous noses. Pegi' was outlawed sometime before in the '30s, but the old timers never let it stop them. There is no limit to the barrage of expletives two angry Indian women on the war-path can contrive, and there was no turning it off once they got started. There was no mention about the LSD Alan Parks and his brothers were selling to us misguided youth. The rules have always been the same. The white guys sell the shit and the Indians get the blame and the addiction. The reason the government doesn't want poor people doing marijuana and LSD is not because of the danger; neither is as addictive as alcohol or heroin. Marijuana does not have the destructive power of whiteman's alcohol and possesses medicinal properties. Edith and Mom went into full-blown protective mother mode. They drove the accusations out the door with whole-hearted, full-throated denial. Not that we were going to tell our mothers the truth; that would have been a fate worse than death. Back then my mom would never have believed I smoked marijuana or was a bad influence.

My brother Chic knew everyone in town; he was a friendly sort of man that most people liked. He easily made friends with strangers. A new barber named Louis Bitz came to town and took over Bart Travis's shop. Bart had found another occupation making more money. Crosby, Stills and Nash's song, *Almost Cut My Hair*, played on KOJM 6.10 radio. It became the hippie anthem of the '60s and barbers almost went extinct. Barber Louis spent his afternoons at the New England, drinking beer and playing pool. Chic couldn't resist challenging a newcomer. The table had a bit of a curve, and Chic won three games of 8-ball. "You gotta be cheatin', you son of a bitch," Louis muttered, and Chic cackled in laughter. "Let's try the table in Kennedy's," Chic offered. They finished their Schlitz beer and chicken, then walked down the street like long lost friends. "Hey, c'mon Oscar…we're just gonna go have a beer and shoot some pool. You're buyin', asshole!" he shouted.

Louis lived outside of town on a farm; he was a bachelor, divorced and alone. Chic invited him over for a home cooked meal. Mom graciously invited him in and offered him a seat at the oak table. He sat on the homemade bench, and she poured him a huge cup of hot black Folgers coffee. He ate two helpings of pinto beans and three homemade biscuits with butter. He mentioned to Chic and my mom that he wanted to rent out the apartment behind the barber shop. It had two bedrooms with running water. This meant a toilet that flushed and a tin shower with a plastic curtain. Plus, the apartment was next to Edith Wall's shack. It was also on U.S. Highway 2, down the street from the Rambler Garage. Edith had five half-black Indian kids. She lived with Jim Earthboy, and they had three more babies in diapers. Edith and my mother feared the welfare department. It was only supposed to be white mothers who got the AFDC benefits, not them.

The streets of Chinook were lively for midweek. The Cozy Corner was packed with groovy long-hair hippie types. The Mopars rumbled in the distance. We drove the 'cruise' in Rick's yellow '67 Dodge Coronet. The 'cruise' was four blocks up and four blocks down Main Street. It was late July, 1969. We talked about the astronauts taking a shit on the moon tonight. It was being broadcast on TV. We were on a mission. Rick slouched behind the wheel, one arm over the steering wheel with a KOOL cigarette burning between his fingers. His curly hair had that 'bed-head' look. It as the '60s and life was groovy. I left to find Jamie Sharples at the Cozy Corner. He had some kick-ass microdot for 50 cents a hit. Jamie was the keyboard player in the Mangold Band. I knew him and Roy Gruss pretty well – they were friends with Victor, of course. Victor was friends with everybody. I completed my *2001 Space Odyssey* delusion, ground control to Major Tom, and waited for Rick to return. "You ready, big guy?" Rick asked, ordering a Dr. Pepper to go. We picked up a 'sixer' at the Elks Bar, the kind on the neon billboard out front with the lady in the martini glass. Rick's parents were out of town in Dallas, visiting Ron, his older brother. He was left to his own devices. We stopped at the Pub to play a game of pool and have a beer. I was only 15, but got served in most bars in Harlem. Georgie Legg at the Servicemen's Bar knew my age and both of my parents. Beanie Hewitt was the proprietor of the world famous Beanie's Tavern. He'd been serving Indians all along, yet we all looked alike to him and he never bothered to check an ID. Grandpa Clyde owned The Pub in Zurich and knew somewhere in his aging mind that I was the same age as Vic, but he served me anyway. "Gawddam kids," he grumbled. "Can't even take a gawddam nap," he complained as he served us Lucky Lager beer and shots of Seagram's 7. Rick and I ordered another sixer to go after we finished our game of pool, feeling the sky grow taller.

We sat in the car, a little buzzed from the July heat and the tranquilized effect of the beer and shots. "Wonder if this shit is any good," I rhetorically pondered as I opened the tinfoil bundle of microdot. "Here…try this," I said as the canary yellow Dodge Coronet staggered out of the parking lot. Jamie always had some kick ass 'electrics' from out of town, and Irv Booth was the keeper of the cross. We laughed and put *Their Satanic Majesties' Request* in the 8-track. *1,000 Light Years from Home* came blasting out of the stock radio speakers at high volume. With a slur and a grin, Rick asserted, "You remind me of a man."

"What man?" I asked.

"The man with the power!" he hauntingly replied.

"What power?" I asked again.

"The power of voodoo," he declared.

"Who do?" I asked, laughing.

"YOU DO, dipshit!" We laughed ourselves silly at the stale acid joke we'd picked up from Irv and Roger.

"Ohhh-kayyy! Here we go!" Putting the Coronet in gear, we weaved out of the parking lot onto U.S. Highway 2 headed east toward Harlem with music blasting, windows down and feeling the rush of the night air. Feeling the coolness of the KOOL menthol cigarette I inhaled then exhaled through my nose, the blue smoke sucked out the open window. Driving up and down the streets of Harlem, we bored easily. Our Junior classmates Emil D'Hooge and John Short were always good entertainment. The acid intensified sound, light and space. Rick suggested, "Let's go see what Alan is up to." "Uh, if you're going there, you better let me off uptown," I replied. "What do you mean? He's my friend," Rick queried. I could feel the microdot taking effect, and I assured Rick it was not a good idea for me to go with him. Rick gave me a puzzled look. He was just Rick, my best friend. He gave me no choice; we stood at the door and Rick knocked. "Hellooo!" Alan said as he opened the door. "It's good to see you…that was a great party at Tab's… shit, you missed a great time." His friendly demeanor disappeared when he saw me standing behind Rick. We stayed long enough to smoke three or four of Alan's joints. Alan Parks was the rich kid in town, and he was obviously quite uncomfortable having an Indian in his parents' house. His 'high context' non-verbal communication screamed, "Get the fuck out of my house. You are not welcome here!"

His parents made their fortune in the hardware business. They, along with most Harlem business owners, had exploited the neighboring Fort Belknap reservation over several generations. Jay Parks was married to Anna, who was the daughter of Eddy Coeurth, or 'Court' as the old traditional Indians called him. The more uncomfortable Alan became, the longer I held to his joint…bogarting and double-toking. Finally, with the microdot coming on heavy, the chroma spectrum of red blended with white superiority. "Hey, big guy…let's go to Boo's and get another sixer," Rick suggested. I was down to my last dollar, but it was a worthy cause. After all, there was no use saving it for tomorrow.

Merle Weere's daughter, Kathy, unexpectedly moved to Missoula with Bill Baker to assume a gig as a security watchman at Hoemer-Waldorf Lumber Mill. Bill with his band, Logna was the rock and roll entrepreneur of Harlem, Montana. The Logna band represented the officialdom of rock and roll: so that meant that Harlem was now in desperate need for something new to gossip about. It was up to us to carry on the tradition of decadence.

Victor was a shoe-in for the open soda jerk position at Merle's Confectionary. Merle took to Victor, trusting him implicitly. I tested him repeatedly. "C'mon Vic…buy me a Coke," I harassed.

"Buy your own fuckin' Coke. Take that last dollar out of your moth-eaten wallet, ya goddam cheap ass Indian," he scoffed.

"Aw, shit…you got a job…all you rich white guys are a bunch of cheapskate dickheads," I jabbed as I dug for the last wrinkled dollar tucked in the recesses of my wallet. "Ok, you win, dammit. I'm thirsty, gimme a Coke," I conceded.

"It's about goddam time, sittin' there takin' up valuable customer space, why I oughta…," feigning a slap on my buffalo-sized head.

"Hey Vic, buy me a burger," I laughed. He shook his head and grumbled.

"Fuck you, Big John, you asshole prick fuckin' son-of-a-bitch… did I forget to mention asshole?"

Our rehearsals were going well, until I saw the smoke coming out of the old black Bandmaster. The smell was familiar – burning transformer. "Oh shit, it's a goner. I'm gonna have to take it to Gruss's to get it fixed. Shit," I muttered. Herb Gruss was Roy's dad, a German immigrant who owned a TV repair shop in Chinook. I liked to hear him talk; his accent sounded like a movie star. "Mr. Gruss?" I called out as I entered his shop. He appeared from behind his workbench, peeking to see who it was from behind the pile of television sets. "I blew up my amp again…need to get it fixed," I confessed. "Chu kits and jour amplifiers and lout music," in his German accent, shaking his head. "Vat dit chu do now?" he asked. I had all four of the Fender amps in for repair at one time or another and bought up his entire stock of 6L6 GE electronic tubes. It was all for rock and roll. He smelled the fried transformer, "It vil be a vile; I am going to have to order a twansfomah," he said. "Uh…a what?" I asked, just so I could hear his accent again. "A twansfomah," he repeated with a grin.

We tried playing two guitars through the remaining Fender Bandmaster. It sucked all the volume out of the 965 AB 763 circuit. The 40 watts just couldn't produce the right feedback squawking I had perfected, which covered my lack of knowing what the shit I was doing. By this point, Vic and I had established ourselves in the greater Harlem locale as the extemporary aficionados of the music business. Without hesitation, without a clue, Victor booked us for every possible opportunity to express ourselves. I broke the news to Victor about the Bandmaster while he was at work slinging burgers and doing the soda jerk. "Damn Vic, we need a new amp. I heard Dale Mailand has his 150-watt Sears for sale…it has six 10" speakers in the cabinet." It was factory made, looked like new, and he was asking $150 for it. "C'mon Victor, I promise I will pay you back this summer when I get my first NYC paycheck." Neighborhood Youth Corp was a work program for poor kids in the inner city. I guess Harlem is about as inner city as you can get.

NYC was a way for us poor kids to earn some beer and weed money in the summer. It was a federal program administered through the Fort Belknap tribes. Jack Plumage was our boss. He went to college at the University of Montana. He was working on an administrative degree…that is when he and Peewee Bigby weren't at the Park Bar. As for his NYC employees, Jack gave little attention to where the hell we were. There were lots of places to hide, giving me time to take naps after eating my 'ring o' red' and commodity cheese sandwiches. 'Ring o' red' was a quasi-Spam-like substance that assured clogged arteries, diabetes and big guts. Most of my friends bought clothes with their NYC paychecks or helped pay for their family's survival, but I was greedy. I spent the government's money on my own adolescent narcissistic Id functions.

"Goddam you, Big John…I should give you this goddam job, and I'll go fuck off like you. So when do you want to go get the son-of-a-bitchin' amp?" Vic asked, with regret for every being my friend.

Chapter 17

19th Nervous Breakdown

It was March, and we moved from Louis Bitz's tiny barbershop apartment – back to the north side, a house next to my cousin, Gordon Azure. It had a real flush toilet and a tin stall shower that leaked into the dirt basement when you used it. The house was probably the first house built in Harlem, 48°31'54N108°47'4" W. It was on the original Main Street, north of the tracks. A city mayor had lived there at one time a hundred years ago. It was now surrounded by three-foot tall dried milk weeds. There was a rusted '48 Hudson and a '36 Chevy randomly dropped in the back yard. The Chevy had two flat tires with weather cracks around each tire. They were probably as old as the car. Various overgrown weeds grew through the floor, and broken glass was strewn about the interior compartment. Beer cans and wine bottles were randomly planted throughout the stand of weeds. The sunbaked prophylactic rubbers were evidence of safe sex. Turquoise paint was chipped from the house siding in patches. Wooden shingles on the roof guided rainwater into the various ceiling leaks throughout the house.

The interior wasn't much better. The same turquoise paint was peeling off the walls in the huge living room. There were no doors on the two bedrooms. Between the bathroom and Mom's bedroom lay the haunted stairwell to the dirt basement. A creepy feeling made it nearly impossible for me to navigate the steps. My native awareness-white buffalo dreams were so different from the experiences of my white friends who descended the stairs, blissfully unaware of what emanations lived there. My brother Chic set up a cot in the corner of the living room. His cot was a wooden door covered with a thin flattened mattress that looked like it had survived a million sleeps. The metal-framed dining room table was surrounded by torn and worn kitchen chairs with the last of the padding falling out in clumps. The kitchen had received no attention since the '40s or '50s, and there were no doors on the cupboards. The age and wear showed plainly; upkeep was nonexistent. On those five wood steps that led to the dirt basement, the ghosts felt the disturbance and reminded me every time I was there alone. I felt them circle around me, warning me not to invade their space with high-volume rock and roll.

The icy chill of winter receded, giving way to the coming spring. Victor was my only real friend; I tried talking to him, but he wouldn't hear any of my depressing intentions. "Fuck Victor, if it weren't for you…I wouldn't have any friends in this fucking school." I grew tired of holding my tongue to the bullshit remarks the white kids spoke audibly enough for me to hear. I didn't want to be around them, and they surely didn't want to be around me. My next-best friends, Charlie and Garth, turned on me. They were teenage assholes but too small in physical stature to harm, and deep down I really didn't want to hurt them. Mostly, I wanted to be friends again, but we were moving beyond that possibility. "Victor, I made up my mind; I have to quit school. I can't take it anymore." Feeling on the edge of suicide, it was as if I was at a psychic juncture from which there was no return, there were no other options.

Victor listened to my story. I didn't fit in with the white friends he had, and I didn't fit in with the other Indian kids. My father insisted I pull myself up by the bootstraps of my moccasins. Could he see the overwhelming cognitive discord that might create? "Whatcha gonna do then?" Tatanka Iyotake asked me. "Damned if I know…I'll find a job," I retorted off the top of my clueless head. I'd made up my mind, sleeping restlessly the night before my sixteenth birthday. Waking to my mother's distant voice calling me by my family nickname. "Brother," her sing song voice called, "It's time to get ready for school!" I got out of bed, pulled on my clothes and staggered to the indoor-outhouse for my morning meditation. Rehearsing my words and wondering if this would be the day, I mustered the courage to tell her my decision. She hummed her endless happy tune, the one that I'd heard since the day I was born. It had no specific melody; you just always knew she was in a happy mood when she crooned. I stood in the middle of the living room. Chic sat on his cot in the corner with his 'sailor coffee'. It could have been used for industrial cleaning solvent.

"You better hurry or you are going to be late for school," my mother insisted. "I'm not going anymore," I blurted. The tune she had been humming stopped in mid hum. "What do you mean you aren't going to school?" she asked, giving me *the look*. Her look made me sink into the cracks in the floor. "I'm quitting school. Ain't learning nothin', and I'm too stupid to understand all their shit. It doesn't matter to anyone anyway," I claimed. "I am never going to use Algebra, but I could use more sleep." I watched her humming tune; it first searched for refuge, then flew out the window. "You get your butt to school right now! I don't want to hear another damn word about it," she ordered with seriousness I'd never heard before. With helpless protest, I left the house to catch up with Victor as he crossed the tracks on the spring trek through the mud to the vile Harlem High School I had come to hate with red passion.

The chill of the short days made it necessary to find a warm place indoors to practice. Gary Parnell joined the band with Victor, Charley and me. We rehearsed religiously until our fingers were near frostbite. It took a while to convince my mother, against my brother Chic's protest. She wanted me to do anything but drink, and the basement was a place she could keep track of me. She was just as protective of all my friends. If I stayed out of trouble, they stayed out of trouble. Despite the protests of the downstairs ghosts, we moved our band equipment into the dirt basement.

I owned all the Fender Bandmasters, even the coveted black amp that Bill Baker used to own. I had paid Leon Mail $125 before Bill told me it was actually his, so I paid him a second time. I owned all the sound equipment and Victor couldn't kick me out of the band again. Gary bought Bill Baker's Gibson ES 335; he was our new 'front man' and singer. The descending 'G' to 'E' chromatic intro, "I'm so Glad, I'm so Glad…," he sang. My Fender Bandmaster turned up to '11', my 1959 ES 350T on '12', I wailed feedback notes as I buried my head in the primitive homemade guitar speaker cabinets. I was engulfed in 'orange sunshine', feeling the heightened aural kaleidoscopic visio-spacial world of Crazy Horse visions. Gary's new position on stage was out in front of the band, Steve Winwood calling him to center stage. The shiny red ES 335 glistened in the pin-wheel Christmas stage light. We did our own version of *G-L-O-R-I-A* with Victor's eclectic drum styling channeling Gene Krupa, Buddy Rich and Keith Moon. I could tell he enjoyed the color orange from the sunny look in his eyes. If it wasn't for Charlie's clockwork bass guitar, we might all have drifted off the planet. He stood rigid without flinching, counting like a Hohner metronome.

The following day the secretary called me into the principal's office during third period study hall. The urgent look on her face spoke volumes as she handed me the phone. It was Chic, and he sounded upset and angry. "Mom is in the hospital. She had a nervous breakdown!" "What do you mean? What happened... where?" I asked. How could this be happening? My thoughts were racing; it was the greatest fear I'd had since Boyd Birch passed away years before. Chic answered, "You guys and your damn racket shaking the house! You know how nervous she gets," he growled with worry. "She is at the hospital...they are keeping her overnight...she's medicated pretty good."

I left without giving notice to the secretary and walked to the county road, toward U.S. Highway 2, then hitched a ride to the hospital. The Fort Belknap Hospital was built in 1878, and it was where I was born. I found Mom there in the hospital bed with the IV stuck in her arm, sedated and drowsy. The nurse informed me "Your mother has suffered a nervous breakdown." That confirmed what Chic had said and ended all the rehearsals in the basement. We were back on the street in search of a place to rehearse.

Leon Main was the new kid in town. He recently moved here from Billings. I heard he played guitar and had been in a rock and roll band before moving to the Highline. We became fast friends. Fun in Harlem was hard to find, options few and far between, so we made our own. It degenerated to stealing plums without getting caught. The coup was good, nobody got busted and we had fresh juicy plums as we patrolled the Harlem streets. That night the boredom was beyond tolerance, driving up and down in Leon's '58 Plymouth. It was faded green with a blue right fender and random rust spots. His car stood out like a sore thumb, a prehistoric dinosaur rolling down Harlem's Main Street. Surely it looked like an armored tank filled with Indians; and we seemed suspicious to 'Bullet Bob' Myers, the county deputy, and Floyd Frye, the local city cop. Obviously all of the town degenerates were isolated on wheels as the two of them scrutinized all who passed, looking for a small town reason to make an official police stop. Leon drove, with Ron Magnuson and Susie Rock beside him. Ron was called Mag by most of his friends. I was in the back seat with Vickie Johnson and 'Bon Bon', whose given name was Yvonne Molina. Bon Bon was visiting and lived in California. We also knew her as 'California Sunshine'; she had a great sense of humor and an exotic, foreign Rocky Boy Chippewa-Cree charm.

Gas was cheap but it didn't matter, we were broke. Conserving fuel, we parked up on the Burlington Northern dock where Jake Kuntz unloaded rail freight from passing shipments bound for either the east or west coast. We'd picked up Susie's sister, Gail, from the Greyhound bus across the street a few hours earlier. She'd just returned from the Rocky Boy pow-wow. These four Indian girls laughed at everything. It was hard to believe we were sober, quite unusual. Who knew it was possible to have fun without our honorary tribal member? It just didn't seem natural. The BN passenger train made its routine 12:34 a.m. stop. Mag had the urge to prove his physical ability. With Susie atop his shoulders, he took off running. We could hear Mag's distinctive laugh as they disappeared into the dark, catching brief glimpses of them running alongside the train in the dim light. We could hear Susie laughing as she knocked on the lighted windows of passengers as they passed.

Like a beacon, the red lights flashed on Bullet Bob's yellow Pontiac from around the 'Money Tree' by the old Chevron station. Behind us, Floyd Frye skidded to a stop in the city cop car. He stirred the dust and gravel, coughing as he leaped out of his police cruiser. He looked like 'Dudley Do-Right of the Mounties' with his .357 Smith and Wesson drawn. "Don't make any fast moves! I have this side covered!" he shouted to Bullet Bob. Bullet had his .38 'hog-leg' semi-trained on Mag and Susie standing in the headlights of his Pontiac. Mag raised his arms, laughing, with Susie still on his shoulders. You could hear their cackles cutting the silence. Susie's hands were held straight in the air, too. Mag grew weak with laughter, his knees about to crumple, as he put Susie down in the gravel. We were all hysterical now, giddy on plum juice. Vickie, Gail and California Sunshine hooted and cackled a Bunty Rock belly laugh. Bunty was Susie and Gail's mother, part Asian, but all Indian to us. We shared poverty and prejudices from the white-privileged people of Harlem.

"Get outta the car…with your hands up," Floyd muttered. He and Bullet shared the thrill of capture. They had in custody the nasty drug dealers that plagued the city. Bullet was at least a half-sheet to the wind; he feigned a look of sobriety as he staggered closer to the light. We rolled out of the car laughing. Floyd pointed the gun directly at me, and the laughter came to a stop in a split second. *These frigging idiots have loaded guns*, I thought as my smile faded. "What were you getting off that train?" Bullet demanded. Mag and Susie looked at each other, showing their empty hands.

"We know you got something off of there," Floyd gasped, now sounding a bit foolish. "Let's search the car," he said, determined to make an official arrest. Bullet staggered closer to us, "What's in the bag?" he demanded, shining his flashlight in Leon's eyes. "Uhhh… plums," Leon said, with a serious look. Bullet grabbed the bag out of Leon's hands, reached in and pulled out a plum, sticking it in his mouth. "We better take these to the lab," he suggested to Floyd. Floyd nodded with his idiotic dumb farmer grin. "Yup, it could be LSD in there," Floyd acknowledged. "Never know," Bullet agreed while pulling another piece of evidence from the bag and placing it in his mouth.

We stood around smoking cigarettes as Harlem's finest rifled through the car. Bullet came out with a crumpled sack that held dirty undies Gail had brought back from her three-day stay at

Rocky Boy. "Sooo…what's in here?" he asked. "Those are mine!" Gail yelped, reaching to grab her brown paper bag. Bullet turned away from her, opened the bag, and sniffed inside…then reached in for the contents. Floyd took the sack from Bob's drunk fingers, taking a sniff of his own as Gail jerked the bag from his hands.

Several cars circled the block, watching the Sunday night excitement and the ensuing drug bust. We waved to them, hooting and hollering. We heard an occasional random outburst of laughter. After a thorough search of Leon's Plymouth, the Harlem police force resigned themselves to failure. Floyd instructed us to stay off the streets. Bullet holstered his gun, frustrated with embarrassment. "You kids better get your asses home," he grumbled in a sideways walk toward his car. Dudley Do-Right had asserted his authority, holstered his gun and withdrawn. Gail retrieved her clothing, arranging the items back in the brown paper bag. She joked, "Damn pervert assholes…geez…what did they think they would find?" Vickie and California Sunshine chimed in, teasing Gail, "Shia! Bullet Bob probably got a thrill. Geez, you'll give the ol' man a heart attack, n'it!" Floyd was another story; his intent was common knowledge. He'd locked himself in the backseat of the cop car with one of the local Indian girls, trapping the two of them and needing help to get out. Townsfolk joked about ol' Joe Whitecow and Floyd fighting over Joe's wife Josephine.

Many reminders of the Indian legacy wandered Harlem like ghosts from bar to bar. White privilege, implicit bias and institutional racism served to keep the Indian in his habituated place. We had many role models to look up to; the walking drunks showed us our Indian pride, our honorary tribal member. *Red shadows*, the children of the blood moon, lurked as reminders for ingrained white guilt – the kind that broken treaties are made of. Joe Whitecow and Josephine were living examples. So were Hambone and Delia, their mules that staggered home when they came to town to drink. Two Gun was another fixture, like a wooden Indian in a black cowboy hat, always standing by the corner of Buttrey's Grocery. The Cuts the Rope boys always got caught with their pants down in the willows behind our five room mansion. Once, one of the women made off with a Cuts the Rope boy's clothes and left him buck-ass naked in the weeds. I traded one of them a drawing for a pair of worn out blue jeans and a pair of old shoes. My cousin Billy Rose was one of the most colorful examples. He drank with my uncles, one of the many feet I saw in the log shack on U.S. Highway 2.

Desperate for a place to practice after my mom's hospital stay, we rented the shack at the junkyard. It was a log cabin that Ron and his brother, Fred Magnuson, built out of used telephone poles. It was one of their father Harold's brilliant ideas. He was experimenting with several avenues to make his entrepreneurial fortune. His big dream was called Bella Vista Heights, and he had plans underway for a model suburban community north of Harlem. The view would overlook the city, with a backdrop of Snake Butte, Three Buttes and the Little Rockies. It was a spectacular view, with the exception of Harlem. Ray and Stella Webb ran the junk yard for H. R. Puff and Stuff Magnuson. They lost their jobs there and vacated the shack as the junkyard dissolved, leaving us to keep the fire going. (Mag) was the guitar player in the band. His dad Harold charged $20 a month to rent the dilapidated log cabin. We left Victor in charge of the details and rent money was never spoken of again. He probably paid it out of his Merle's paycheck. He knew we were irresponsible, above the responsibility of being accountable. We were in search of the unknown perfect Pete Townsend cosmic chord.

Mag played a new Epiphone double pick-up solid body guitar. Pete Townsend was his idol rock and roll guitar player. He practiced leaps and mastered the 'windmill' guitar thrashing, emulating his hero. Mag wasn't that good of a guitar player, but nobody had the same royal Canadian heart. He was far better than me; I certainly was no Montana Slim. We practiced regularly at the log shack. It became our home away from home a mile from town. We listened to rock albums so loudly that the cops came to chew us out. Mag wrote a new symphony for a rock and roll orchestra. The crescendo rose in intensity, *Air on the E-String.* It was reminiscent of Vanilla Fudge or Mag's favorite Bach recording. He did a windmill, then a leap…dropping to the floor with a squawk of feedback from his amplifier. With another passionate leap, he jumped headfirst into the center-pole that held up the roof. After shaking off the concussive effect, we continued cautiously, Mag subdued without further leaps and windmills. Victor stayed the course, kicking over his mismatched double bass drum set as Keith Moon smiled on.

The eastern world was exploding, the Viet Nam War escalated and my friends were drafted, leaving us without a replacement guitar player. Mag was the first to receive his draft notice. He mournfully sold me his 1959 Gibson 350T big blonde guitar. It was the guitar I had coveted, watching him play with Bill Baker at the meat-market practice place. Mag was off to basic training at Fort Hood. Leon's younger brother, Kenny Main, graduated from high school in Lodge Grass and had spent a year at the Billings Automotive Training program. He worked at Boo's Conoco with Victor. He tested the waters with the evil capitalist establishment he swore against. Victor, Kenny and I attempted learning the songs I wrote. They were even too complicated for me to comprehend. We were near extinction; I all but lost confidence in my fading guitar fantasy. Mag's and Leon's musical superiority were light-years beyond my capacity, means and motivation. They played with the assurance and confidence of Jimi Hendrix and Carlos Santana. I did not.

Chapter 18

Werneke-Korsekoff Syndrome

The light was dim in the distance as we searched under the rocks at the home of unreachable dreams, Bella Vista Heights. The place was familiar after months of covert secrecy. The party was starting and all our parents were home safe in bed or at the bar. Leon and I found the rock where we stashed our acid. He took out seven hits of microdot and handed them to Larry. "Hang on to these a second," he said. "How many should I take?" Larry asked. "Shit no…don't take any of those!" Leon exclaimed. "Oh geez…fuck no…gimme those!" I said, taking them from his hand. We watched out for Larry; he was Gary's little brother and had been epileptic during his early childhood. He wanted to be a degenerate like his brother and the rest of us. Gary Parnell was in the army, stationed in the jungle of Panama. He'd been gone almost a year already, and we rarely heard from him. Leon replaced the LSD in its container beneath the rock. We got in his old '58 Plymouth, and drove the mile and a half back to the log cabin at the junkyard. Leon and Emil popped the cork in the keg from Kennedy's Bar, and there was plenty of firewood to burn in the old cast-iron wood stove. We were set for the night. Leon had just gotten a new phonograph needle for his turntable. He had also bought The Who's new *Tommy* album before he came back from winter quarter at Eastern Montana College.

Leon wanted to go into the service. Elmer Main insisted his son be spared from the lifetime of nightmares he'd brought home from 'code talking' during WWII. At his dad's insistence, Leon went to college to stay out of Viet Nam. Leon was a sensitive spirit, he lacked the Ego strength for war, not that any of us had the heart to kill. Leon's younger brother, Kenny, was of a different temperament. He generally annoyed Leon with his sophistication, amoebic logic and flexibility. On the other hand, our two most enigmatic band members, John Short and Emil D'Hooge, kept it entertaining with their absurd humor. Besides, Emil was friends with Jamie Sharples, and he had all the good acid. There were a few other hangers-on who made our musical home complete. Our friendships were solid for the most part.

Victor was still part of the band, but he had to babysit most nights so his parents could go to drinking meetings at the VFW. The LSD was distributed in ceremonious fashion…John Short, Emil, Kenny, me, and finally Leon. Marlin Norheim and Larry Parnell were buddies. They travelled together, but were only allowed to drink beer and smoke other peoples' weed. Marlin was tall and skinny with blond hair. His nickname was Banana Man – Emil gave him the name after an LSD hallucination. Larry was stocky and built for pulling a plow. He wanted to be part of the music crowd. We goaded and teased him until he eventually sprang for a six pack once. He always made sure that he drank at least six beers, if not more. We knew better than to give Marlin and Larry acid for fear of sending them too far into orbit. Marlin took a hit off the chenupa, inhaling the pegi' deeply. "Catch me, Big John. I got a weak mind," he said, falling over backwards. I stood in front of him as he went over. We debated at length the meaning of *Tommy*, and the implications of this new musical concept.

The acid took effect; Leon's words melted into the dim green light dripping down the log walls. Leon prophesied Jimi Hendrix was going to come down on a comet, like a blazing star that lived and died in a blink of an eye, leaving his imprint on the American psyche for generations to come. It was obviously the ravings of a madman on acid. As I looked into Leon's face, the curls of his long hair turned to demonic horns. His smile was of the devil. I yelled, "Holy shit!" Leon laughed, "Whhhat?" *Whoooaaa*...I thought as Leon morphed back into himself. The conversation continued. "Jimi, Janice and Jim Morrison were like the three disciples. They were here to show us the new way...now they're gone." I hung onto every word Leon said, certain that he had some mystic secret to the universe. Just like the Nostradamus guy Emil quoted, debating that the end of times would consist of aliens and blowjobs.

Emil wasn't always focused on the absurd, he was a man of social conscience. We debated the roles of the establishment bourgeoisie and the Marxist proletariat class. This week was like any other week. After a weekend of degenerate beer drinking and LSD tripping, we returned to school for our weekly indoctrination of propaganda. The Viet Nam War heated up; there were marches all over the country. We heard the news that four college students at Kent State in Ohio were killed by the U.S. National Guard for protesting the war. We saw Kent State as the rally cry for hippie rebellion. It was a call to action that we could not resist. Emil was the juvenile leader for a juvenile alcoholic resistance of our own. Within hours, students were called to protest. Emil at the heart of the movement. It was the wonder years, a new decade and a time for change. Emil tossed away his white privilege to accept his INDIAN heritage. He was part Chippewa, Turtle Mountain Indian, I think, although we never discussed it and he was never questioned. He was Hank D'Hooge's son, and that was good enough for me. My dad worked for him before Hank died, leaving Jean, his wife, to raise five sons alone. Rick and Eddy were already grown with lives of their own. Emil's other brothers were still in school. Terry was a couple years older and Patrick was the youngest. Emil fulfilled his youthful destiny as an indian and leader of the Harlem Hippie Rebellion.

Inside our band cabin we heard Alice and Grandma Sarah's voices; we were stupefied in surprise and shock. Victor opened the door, stepping into the log cabin ahead of his mother and grandma. "See, I told you there wouldn't be anything going on here, just drinkin' a few beers," Victor explained. Alice and Sarah came in, looking around at the disrepair, the lack of upkeep – not a sign of a mop or a broom. Short stammered and stuttered, "Wo… wo…would you like a beer?" "All we have is Lucky Lager." Emil remarked, "We were just going to get a keg if you wanna wait." "No…that's ok, we don't want to bother you boys. Be careful and don't be driving around…the cops are out tonight," Sarah said, with Alice concurring. "We'll make sure Victor gets home safe. We'll just stay here tonight, probably," Emil assured. They left into the night, headlights bouncing off toward Highway 241, each with a newly opened beer in her hand.

The acid was coming on, lights flickered with the familiar aural sparkle. The ocular disturbance created tangential cracks in the cosmic egg. My thoughts transcended physical awareness between this world and the other, where everything was not solid, but floated on air like a ghost in the mist. I withdrew to the center of existential being to the void of nothingness. I teetered as I stood, feeling as if my knees floated off the planet with every step. *Man, Sharples has some good shit…maybe I took too much. What if I never come down…wouldn't that be a trip?* I continued gazing into Leon's homemade strobe light. It was a wooden box with an electric fan motor. He had taped a cardboard wheel to the motor with a hole in one edge to let light flash through the disc. It was originally one of Bill Baker's ingenious inventions. "Victor…here, you better take this hit and catch up," I said, giving him the option. "Gimme a beer," he said, tossing down the hit of Orange Sunshine and washing it down with half a can of Lucky Lager.

It was Midwinter Fair on the Fort Belknap Reservation, and there were Indians from everywhere. They came because they were Indian. It didn't matter if they had money, they got by somehow, used to living from moment to moment, day by day. Change and being uprooted is their history; they know nothing else. They have been uprooted since the white invasion, but that is another story. They came from Rocky Boy, Fort Peck, Browning, and even a few from Crow. The winter roads were terrible, closed from Billings north to Fort Belknap. We huddled up at the practice place on the hill, rehearsing a song Leon learned called *Whiskey Bread*. Someone arrived, and the interruption was welcomed in the monotony of the 'A minor' progression. "Hellooo boys…I want you to meet my friend. This is Floyd Westerman…Floyd Redcrow Westerman. He's a singer…he's gonna sing at the pow-wow tomorrow. He needs to use your guitars and amplifiers… the Bureau will pay you," Elmer rambled on, taking pride in the introduction of his new acquaintance. Elmer Main was Kenny and Leon's father. He was the BIA Superintendent at Fort Belknap.

We stood there looking at each other, agreeing with Elmer. It might rub off; we could be his backup band on the road to Indian fame and fortune. Floyd was a guest for Midwinter Fair; he was a motivational speaker. I could tell he had motivated and inspired Elmer this evening – he was in a fine mood. Elmer and Floyd weaved and wobbled in the green light, obviously two and a half sheets to the wind, cheeks flapping in the breeze. "Hey, you guys mind if I sing one with you?" Floyd asked, reaching for my

Gibson guitar. "Hey brother, this is sure a nice guitar…can I use this one?" he asked, staggering in front of the microphone. He tapped out a basic Hollywood Indian beat in E minor and started singing, "B…I…AAAA, we don't want your white man way… hay yahhh hayyy yahhhh." The band played along, "Hay yahhh hayyy yahhhh." Floyd left with my guitar and our new speakers. He continued drinking his motivation. The brazen drunk Indian knocked our speakers off the stage as his drinking continued. Those speakers were never repaired as Elmer had promised. The Bureau of Indian Affairs showed me again that it's promises were not to be believed as the Coyote lurked behind us. Floyd Redcrow Westerman's song soon became a sounding cry for AIM the American Indian Movement in 1968. It garnered him drunken Indian celebrity status as an actor and spokesperson.

Chic was the dreaded authoritarian in the family after his return from the navy. I was going through my identity stage, filled with cognitive dissonant introjections and projections, the neural pathways so deeply entrenched in my pliable, LSD soaked brain, the stains may never be erased. My father was never available; he lived in his painful World War II grief, saturated with PTSD memories. Chic drank daily to supplement his chronic barbiturate and insidious narcotic addiction. His several back surgeries substantiated his use. The IHS hospital handed drugs out freely with each cut of the surgical blade. He and I were beyond communication in his mental state. It was a battle of wills – he threw my chenupa and pegi' to the wind; while my mother retrieved it without his knowledge. It was rebellion time in my personal life and across the nation. Martin Luther King, the promoting of Malcom X 's black supremacy and it was all significant for the human beings. The white man felt he'd given up so much to these indigents, interlopers in their America. To calm the storm included in the Civil Rights Act before congress they had added the Indian Civil Rights. The white government had become fearful of the American Indian Movement, they felt it was a threat to national diplomacy and again they had given up so much already. They attached a rider to the bill making it unlawful to travel somewhere to join a protest, or in their words a 'riot', doing their best to stop the Indian from a modern day Ghost Dance.

Every time my sister, Annette, came to visit, she bragged about all of the great things she'd done since we'd seen her last. The AIM movement in South Dakota was causing a stir at Wounded Knee. Giving rebellious fodder to the stories of her Seattle AIM friends, my mother rolled her eyes as Annette asserted her authority. My niece, Doll, sat in complete silence as her mother went on about Jerry – she was so proud that he was doing well in Miles City. It almost made me wish I was locked up with him. He was in reform school for three years. I got a couple letters, the last one was two years before. He didn't sound like the kid I knew, he had become very hard and angry at the world; he was too young to have that kind of anger. My sister had beat him for things he did and didn't do. After a while he just took the beatings because they were offered. He stopped feeling the pain that came with them. Even Doll became hardened without Jerry to protect her. She learned to fend for herself the way her mother taught her. My sister was prideful yet critical of everything she herself had taught her children.

The American Indian Movement was a good idea in concept, however it was flawed from the beginning, run by wounded and traumatized Indians. We all know that no three Indians can agree on anything. That's why there are Indians still living on reservations. The Fort Belknap chapter of AIM was run by the Main family. They were Leon and Kenny's militant cousins. Mostly they drank Lucky Lager beer and Seagram's 7. It was the honorary tribal member that guided their convictions. They mainly reacted to their own alcoholic whims. Like the night they shot up the Harlem Police Department – they had no purpose, no warrior intent. They were pretty much run out of town; there were a few breaths of fear, but mostly laughter. Indian civil rights hinged on black civil rights. There might never have been an Indian civil rights movement if not for Martin Luther King, Jr. and Malcolm X. The fear of white exposure for the atrocities of the continuing genocide gave way to appeasement of the Indian nations, but armed resistance in South Dakota could not be tolerated. Nixon was digging in quicksand; the Indian uprising had to be silenced, and Leonard Peltier was martyred without hesitation.

While the tension at Wounded Knee escalated, our band reached acclaim in the far-east. Victor got us a gig almost 300 miles away in Plentywood, Montana. We were unstoppable with our great white leader. It was in the northeastern corner of the state, near Canada and North Dakota. He had a knack for getting us into the impossible. "Victor…how the fuck we going to get there?" I asked. "We'll figure it out when the time comes. Don't worry… this is our chance. Oh yeah, the theme song is *Precious and Few*… we have to learn it. Anyone know it?" he asked. Kenny was the mechanic, so he was in charge of transportation. Eddie Halver was searching for his identity; he offered to haul the equipment in his '59 International pickup. Otto Shaeffelmaeir insisted we use his '62 Ford Galaxy, and Victor had his new '68 Rambler. Kenny and Otto gave the vehicles a final inspection before we headed east on U.S. Highway 2 towards Malta. That was the farthest east I had ever ventured since Kenny and Leon had lived in nearby Frazier years before when their dad was school superintendent there.

We drove past Malta, dissecting Casey Kasem's *American Top 40* on the radio. We listened to the countdown; it was up to Leon to get us out of this jam. *Precious and Few* by Climax came on the radio. We all groaned, cussing at Victor who drove in front of our little convoy, cruising in his Rambler, oblivious to our rancor. "I like that song. It's a good slow dance song," Otto positively interjected into our guffaw. We pulled into Glasgow and stopped for gas, all of us climbing out of the car to confront Vic. "Victor, you asshole. We can't do this song… what the fuck we gonna do?" I growled. He didn't say anything as he went in to pay for the gas. We lined up at the Standard Oil pisser like hillbillies on parade. John Short and Terry D'Hooge sparred in the parking lot. Emil grinned, sitting in the back seat rolling pegi' sticks. Victor came out of the station with a smile of relief on his face. "Look what I found! Climax on 8-track! We can figure out how to play this while we're driving…it should work!" "I can take the player out of the car…we can use your battery if you got a wrench," Kenny suggested.

We pulled up at the school unaware of our lack of cool. Victor's '68 Rambler didn't do much to impress the senior class president. He drove a cherry red '70 Chevelle. Eddy Halver sat in his International dinosaur, trying to look cool in his Boo's Conoco sunglasses. Otto and Terry searched out the girls in jeans hanging prom decorations. They flipped their blond hair, noses high in the air, and laughed at Terry and Otto dressed in their plaid short-sleeve shirts. Plentywood is a wealthy Republican community. Most of its inhabitants inherited family farms from their grandparents who lived and died fighting the savage Indians. The Nakoda temporarily occupied their land for 'one thousand moons', waiting for the rightful white privileged owners to claim what was not theirs. Like the prairie blight, they came in hoards across the virgin grassland in war surplus Conestoga wagons.

Leon ground out *Whiskey Bread, I'm So Glad* and *Voodoo Chile'* on his Gibson SG. We followed along like we had practiced, projecting our audio-visual, LSD soaked neural pathways of psychedelic images. The prom king and queen were announced. They looked like sugar figurines on top of a Hollywood wedding cake. The Prom Court started singing to accompaniment played on a pristine Fender Rhodes piano, "*Precious and few are the moments we two can share...*" The royalty danced slowly, he humping her leg, she humping his. It was absolutely beautiful...the crowd cheered. Then the masse humping began as the entire audience mounted the dance floor. After the song finished, we continued our performance. The finale was a 15-minute version of *G-l-o-r-i-a,* followed by *Louie Louie* and *Johnny B Good*, before we fizzled out altogether. We drove through the night and got home in the early hours of the morning just as the sun peeked over a crimson cloud. Victor was anxious to share his valiant adventure to his betrothed, decked out in their heart and letter jackets.

Weeks later, after Victor and his girlfriend's breakup, we drove around most of the night in Rick's Dodge Coronet, first to Hogeland to get a case of Lucky Lager. We knew better than tobreak out the Seagram's 7 with Vic in this emotional state." We drank that by the time we got back to Harlem. The Dodge started to stagger by the time we reached Zurich. Kim Funk shattered Victor's heart when she went off with that no account Tunce Messerly. He drove a red '74 Bonneville with huge letters in red and white-checkered contact paper on the side. It read, 'Tear em up Tunce'. In his drunkenness, Victor vowed to kick his ass for stealing his woman. He tried to get out of the car when he saw Tunce parked at the Harlem rest home where Kim worked. Rick pulled him back into the car, "Get your ass in here, you fucking moron. You're going to get hurt! He'll kill you! Besides, you're too drunk to fight, you idiot!"

I laughed at the thought of Victor fighting; neither of us had done much of it since we were kids. Back then, Jerry and I used to save Vic's ass from the Azure cousins. I was always fighting one of my Indian friends who wanted to pick on Victor. There was nothing we could do to fight this battle for him. His drunken tenacity overruled practical logic; he was determined for the sake of love to kill the bastard. We sat north of Zurich, drinking common sense by the six pack. Vic got out and started to walk. Refusing all reason, he wanted to fight. He took a couple misguided swings when Rick tried to steer him back to the car. Rick grabbed to steady him, but he fought on. Wrestling him to the ground, Rick and I held him upside-down over the edge of the bridge until he promised to stop fighting. We weren't the enemy, and the enemy would kill him for pure entertainment.

Emil got us a gig for the Carter Harvest Community Festival. Joan Jordan was the entertainment committee's 16-year-old chairwoman. Emil talked about her incessantly; if I hadn't known better, I'd have said he was infatuated. We took a new approach to booking our band – we put Emil in charge. The gig was scheduled for the end of October, right after harvest and before Halloween. Otto was our reliable transportation. He wanted to get to Great Falls to see Lana Winters; she had moved to Great Falls, leaving Otto with the lovesick blues. We did the last rehearsal of Jimi Hendrix and Alice Cooper hits before packing our mismatched equipment for the gig. Leon thought it looked groovy with all the funky worn out cabinets, just like the *Hit Parader* magazine photos.

We got to the log shack early the next morning anticipating getting on the road before noon. Kenny drove his red '63 Plymouth Fury. It was a good war pony. Otto and Terry tied seven used spare tires to the top of Otto's '59 Chevy van. "Don't worry… we'll use them all before we get back," Otto grinned. "Yeah, they're throwaways," Terry laughed. We loaded the equipment into the van. Victor and I rode in the van with Otto and Terry, and we stopped to pick up John Fish. He had the pegi' for the ride. Kenny, Leon, Emil and John Short piled in the Plymouth Fury. Sonny was waiting at his stucco shack for Kenny to pick him up. We made it past Chinook without a flat. We approached Pork Chop Hill when the left rear tire blew. Otto and Terry went into action like an Indianapolis 500 pit crew. Otto jacked up the van while Terry unstrapped the first spare tire. Otto removed the flat while Terry put the spare in place, and they screwed and tightened the lugs in a single fluid movement.

We stopped at Clyde's In and Out as we pulled into Havre. One more stop at Northern Electronics for guitar strings, then out to the junction on U.S. 87 South. We were south of Loma before the second tire went, and the force of the blowout almost ran us off the road. Fish and I sat in the van, savoring the taste of homegrown pegi'. He grew it at his grandpa Herb's place in Lodge Pole. John was in the Johnson-O'Malley program for poor Indian kids. The government paid for him to live with Henry Miller's family and go to school in town. He had been orphaned, then raised by grandparents after his parents were killed several years earlier in a tragic accident. He didn't like to talk about it. Otto and Terry changed the tire in record time with Victor's expert supervision. We arrived at the Carter Community Hall in the middle of the afternoon, right behind Kenny's fast horse, the Plymouth Fury.

Emil and Victor went off to find Joan Jordan so we could get set up. Otto was anxious to get to Great Falls to see Lana. She was waiting for him, in spite of her father's discouragement – she could do much better. Vic and Emil came back after several minutes. There were farmers and farmers' wives hauling straw bales, folding tables, pumpkins and corn stock decorations. Emil reported that we couldn't set up yet. When Kenny asked why, Victor scoffed, "We can't set up until after the fuckin' cake walk." Otto announced, "I'm headed for Great Falls…get in." Kenny chimed in, "Let's go then…I'll follow you in case you blow another tire." We were in the big city. Despite the intimidation of traffic lights and one-way streets, we finally reached downtown Great Falls on Central

Avenue. Leon looked like George Harrison crossing Abbey Road. We walked up and down Central in awe of the high rise three and four-story buildings.

We stopped at Tracey's Café on the west end of Central. Everyone ordered burgers and fries and watched the city scene through the big plate glass window. This was as good as Merle's Confectionary. I'd never seen so many strange faces in one place. Victor told the waitress his life story; she was old as his mom, but she listened. He went on about playing in Carter. The waitress grinned, "Oh my, you boys are a long way from home, aren't' you?" John and I let Victor do most of the talking…that's what white guys do best. John stuttered, "W-w-we-we are from Harlem." I was still buzzed from the pegi', so I just nodded and grinned. She shook her head, gathering the dirty dishes and the dollar tip. She put the tip in her pocket, "Thank you gents, and play pretty at the dance." We walked east on North 1st Avenue. Otto pulled up and honked just as we approached the courthouse.

The return route was an hour north on U.S. 87 to Carter. When we arrived the parking lot was full, and the festivities had already begun. The farmers were in their Sunday best with new plaid cowboy shirts, Stetson hats and Tony Lama boots everywhere. The wheat harvest of the Nakoda homeland was obviously plentiful. There were no buffalo visible, only miles of grain and the industrial mechanical machines that feed America. It was the Choteau County tradition that everyone owns the latest 1971 Ford truck, not to be outdone by Chevy or Dodge. Emil and Victor went to discuss the final logistics with Joan, anticipatory grief calling if Rita ever found out his felonious intent. Rita Rasmussen had already laid claim to him, he just didn't know it yet. They returned and guided us to a side door – all musicians are let in through the side door for some reason. The stage curtain was closed, and we had the stage to ourselves. We were ablaze with keenness for certain success.

The master of ceremonies announced the final activity of the evening. The cakewalk was the main event of the festivities. It was a plantation slave's walk of grace with a bucket of water balanced on his head. Where in the hell these white Scandinavian farmers assimilated this strange ritual into their local mores was somewhat puzzling. The announcer introduced the contestants, and the crowd hooted and hollered when the winner was proclaimed. John Short had the curtain rope in his hands as the announcer introduced the band. "And now for your evening's entertainment. Let's hope they know a polka and a shoddish. Uh…Logna…from Harlem," the MC read, lacking any enthusiasm. Short opened the stage curtain, and Leon went into *Voodoo Chile*, his Bandmaster amp on eleven and a half. The sea of cowboy hats exited like a tide of rednecks looking for a pig to pork.

The Jimi Hendrix rendition ended with screeching guitars and a three-and-a-half-minute cymbal crash. "Helllloooo everybody… we're LOGNA from Harlem," Victor's voice rang out, looking over a sea of youthful faces. The evening was flawless thanks to our pegi' traditions and some really good hashish Leon brought from 'Billins'. Billings was the college town, a mecca for progressive thinkers like us. Emil was a success with Joan. He was the coolest, and he took advantage of his glory. We got paid in cash…a total success. Victor took the expenses off the top – gas and three used tires. We split the rest equally. I pocketed the $18.52 and had enough money for cigarettes, alcohol and a bag of pegi'. Otto and Terry changed the fifth flat as we loaded the van for our long 110-mile voyage home. I sat admiring their technique as they changed the last spare in front of the Spa Bar in Zurich.

Chapter 19

A Legacy In The Making

At last, senior year came into full view the fall of 1971. Victor and I had come a long way together since 1957. Our lives were shaped by the harsh and critical introjects and projection of our alcoholica families, our teachers, and rock and roll. We forged confluential friendships with Johnny Rodriguez, Floyd Westerman and Joe Whitecow. Emil, Kenny, Leon, Rick, Mag, Gary, the Baker family, and a whole host of characters were of significant influence. There were heroes like Soak Miller who now owned Beanie's Bar. Other role models like Grandpa Clyde, Jay, Uncle Dempsey, Babe, Byo and my dad taught us the reality of life, shaping our values and beliefs. There was a plethora of extended family, friends and a few of the south siders who provided rejection and criticism. The web of life became a five-dimensional ecosystem; thoughts swirled through this existential awareness of my place in this idiopathic, corrupted developmental stage – a formal operational stage filled with doubt and theoretical conjecture.

The band's acclaim spread from Thackery's garage through Phillips County. Several babies were conceived behind the old weather beaten bus garage, a legacy in the making. We were beside ourselves with exhilaration when Victor told us that Malta High School had chosen us over *Yellowstone* for their fall homecoming dance. It wasn't necessarily because we were better, in fact I'm sure that Victor undercut their price by several hundred dollars. As the day of the gig approached, we were in dire straits. There was no pegi' anywhere in white or red America. Arty left for the summer and hadn't returned yet; maybe he never would. We did know it was a scarce commodity even before the white jocks and cowboys discovered the medicinal healing power of the pegi' spirit, and it was even more elusive now. We filled Leon's old '55 Buick at the Texaco station and shared our grievance with Irv Booth, who listened intently to our woes, then disappeared to the tire shop. He returned momentarily with a wicked grin, "I don't have much, but this might help you out," he said, handing Leon two small pinners. We thanked him profusely, knowing it was a pitifully futile but generous gesture.

Irv Booth was a psychology student at Northern Montana College, an ad hoc member of the Havre social elite. He surely had access to the best pegi' that only he could find in Havre. Far be it for me to question his generosity. We arrived in Malta with ample time to set up our equipment. We had two Fender Bandmasters and a Fender Tremolux amplifier for guitars and bass. I had three mismatched Electro-Voice microphones that had long ago been discarded by Bill and Rick. We used a Fender Bandmaster with the three antique high-impedance microphones. Our light system consisted of the two 100-watt colored pinwheel Christmas lights that Grandma Sarah had given us years before. Yellowstone was a semi-regional band that had played with Paul Revere and the Raiders. It was delusional to think we were competition. They had the latest state of the art equipment and a polished act, but we were much cheaper. We were out-classed, out-staged, and Victor's gift of gab had once again gotten us into this jam. Blindly, a band of fools, we followed Victor's lead like morons to a standardized IQ test.

After setting up the equipment in the Malta High School gym, we retreated to Kenny's '68 Charger near the rear of the building. We prayed to the pegi' spirits for a successful performance, and possibly the addition of a small miracle. Irv's generosity was given appropriate appreciation with every draw off those scanty joints. Vic abstained, but I inhaled deeply into my psyche as my thoughts merged with my Crazy Horse vision. We finished the pegi', wishing for more. We had a half hour to tune up before the homecoming gala festivities began. My head floated in a fluid, echoing chords of confluential harmonic overtones. I knew there was an 'E' note in there somewhere. I watched as Leon's bottom tones literally rolled across the floor, falling short at my feet. "Oh shit…I'm really fucked up…what the fuck?!" the thought echoed in my pineal head space. It passed across my eyelids like a neon banner alerting the media. The only thing I could do was beg Leon to bail me out. Maybe if I left my amp on '1' nobody would notice.

Victor counted, "1…2…3…4." I came in somewhere in between while watching the number '4' circle the stage, chase the '2', then stumble over the '3'. Victor's face turned several shades of green and purple under the blue Christmas pinwheel light. He as our drummer was the only one who was consciously able to function. Leon registered a look of intense panic as he struggled to find the notes on the fretboard. Leon played guitar left-handed and upside down anyway, which made this situation all the more confusing. The notes looped around my head like mosquitoes, dive bombing from 100 feet across the stage. Kenny stood like a rock in his stoic Indian pose. It was falling apart before our very eyes. The night degenerated from there, a memory we long to forget. Irv's generosity was our demise. The white man pegi' was a coyote trick laced with angel dust, which explained the devil's smile that came with 'Iktome's gift'. It was then that I remembered Irv's wave on our way out of town, smiling a coyote grin as we passed.

High school graduation neared, following New Years of 1972. The bookkeeping instructor, Mr. Murch, warned me that unless I completed the bookkeeping project I wasn't going to graduate. I had never been good at math and was usually less interested in school than most. My interest was more with fulfilling the expectation of becoming the town drunk. I was off to a good start – I had been in training all my life. There was the full catalog of episodes from childhood, watching my relatives, my brothers and my father drink their way to dysfunction.

I complained to Victor, "Hell. I shoulda quit when I wanted. I'm not gonna fuckin' graduate anyway. My mom is gonna be really pissed," I moaned. "So whatcha gonna do…quit?" he asked. I thought about that as a viable option; I could walk out now and fulfill all the stereotypes. I pondered the benefits of being shitfaced drunk by midnight. Leon and Kenny usually picked me and Emil up after school. We paid homage to the sanctity of the chenupa, to the pegi' spirits. "If I have to go through this shit, so do you," Victor asserted. "You are gonna pass this gawddam class if I have to kill you. You ain't getting off that easy…I'll kick your ass all the way to your shoulder blades!" Every day after that Victor harassed and harangued me to finish the bookkeeping project, even though I had no clue what I was doing. Single entry…double entry… ledgers…who gives a shit? I wondered how Leon, Kenny and Emil were enjoying our afterschool ceremony.

I was to graduate from Harlem High School with the class of 1972, 50th out of a class of 52…only two other students did worse than me. I wasn't sure how that could possibly be, but I didn't have much time to care. It was time to explore my future successful endeavors, spending time with my friends drinking at the Harlem Hill log house practice shack.

My mother was there to see me graduate, along with both Victor's parents. My dad was at Kennedy's Bar keeping a bar stool warm. After the commencement ceremony, Victor and I stopped to say hello to our dads on our way to the kegger. We'd already had several beers and a few shots of Seagram's 7 before entering the bar and the LSD trailers were just beginning. There they were, my dad and Jay, nursing their beers like they'd finished a failed harvest. Victor boomed, "We want to buy these ol' duffers a beer for all they've done." I didn't say anything, ambivalent about drinking with my father. Shafter winked, then went about setting up another round for our dads. Leaving Kennedy's, we realized that the graduation party had left without us. We spent an hour driving around on the prairie north of Harlem. We approached the headlights of another lost graduate; it was too late to retreat when the red light of the police cruiser came on. "You lost?" came a voice from behind the flashlight. "We're looking for the kegger," Victor answered. Chuck Shillings poked his head in the window of the '68 Ford pickup. Flashing his red-headed grin he said, "Follow me… it's this way."

My mother moved to Spokane the day after graduation. I never noticed that she was sick with thyroid cancer. I was too deeply immersed in my own narcissism. She didn't want to worry me with her troubles. I spent the first summer of adulthood working on the Baker farm. Rick had recently returned from the war. He drank like a fish, sharing stories of drinking in Viet Nam. He went on with his life like the war had no effect on him. His smile was gregarious and he kept a cheerful persona in spite of memories that must have surrounded him. Rick and I worked all week with nasty hangovers from the night before. Fortunately, we were fine by quitting time and drove twenty miles of gravel road to resume our drinking. We drank a lot of 'Animal Beer' and R&R whiskey. I was articulate and sophisticated as a professional drinking man. I must say I was very good at it.

It was a dubious time for most young men's futures in 1972. The Viet Nam conflict was in full eruption with live TV footage shown daily on the evening news with Walter Cronkite. I was way overweight with flat feet, so I had no chance of being drafted. All I was good for was a target. I also had a strong aversion to guns and killing animals, let alone people. Shortly after graduation the news broke of the Watergate scandal. The Republican Party was caught red handed trying to break into the Democratic National Headquarters. The Nixon administration denied involvement, and five of his most expendable henchmen were arrested and charged with the crime. Cronkite gave daily updates – the country was in chaos. There was nobody you could trust; the days of reliable and valid politics were days of the past. Corruption trickled down from the highest to those of us on the lowest order. Peace officers suddenly became law enforcers, and criminals got sneakier, committing only one crime at a time. President Nixon was re-elected in the fall, one lie at a time.

When we were too hung over to go to the bars, we listened to the Baker family entertain themselves with stories and memories. Ol' Ed sat in his antique rocking chair smoking unfiltered Camel cigarettes. His fingers were stained from years of storytelling. He always mixed truth with humor, sometimes they were synonymous. We watched the sinking sun, drinking Animal Beer after a hard day's harvest. The conversation was short, mostly grunting. "Yep… nope…maybe," were profound statements. We talked about Elvis and the Beatles; we hashed over the merits of Jerry Lee Lewis and Elton John. "Why hell, I remember when these guys played…Bill, Leon, and Gary Parnell…you were there," Ol' Ed said, looking at Rick with a nod and pointing with his lips, the motion obscured as

I took a drink. Ed reminisced, "I thought these guys were headed for the Ed Sullivan show. By God, they were pretty damn good."

Ed continued slowly rocking as the ashes of his Camel grew longer. "Now by golly, ol' Gramma Baker…she was the best dang piano player in the Milk River Valley. She played for all the weddings and for the church on Sundays," he drawled in an easy voice, the memory reflected in his eyes. "Well, one day little Freddie Baker was taking piano lessons from Gramma, sittin' right next to her on the piano stool. In the middle of the lesson, she had a bad case of gas…musta ate something that didn't agree too well. The piano piece came to a booming crescendo as Gramma passed a thunderous flatulence into the air." He went on with the story, "*The Maiden's Prayer* suddenly retarded to the normal pianissimo volume. Poor Freddie crinkled his nose, his eyes watering and fighting for air. Gramma gloriously concluded the song with brazen olfactory denial and a look of success in her eyes. When Freddie recovered enough to ask her the name of the piece, Gramma's wit kicked in and she said, '*The Storm*! Did you like it?' Hell…Freddie wrinkled his nose, still fighting back gaseous tears and claimed, 'Well, it was okay, but I didn't like the part where the lightnin' struck the shit house!'"

The whole room broke into laughter and sarcastic fart jokes took flight. The church-key rhythm of Animal Beers opening accompanied the humor. Even Bob finally cracked a smile, and for him it was a rare occurrence. Ed pulled the pack of Camels out of his shirt pocket, lighting a new one from the embers of the cigarette in his fingers. It had burned to ash while he told his gramma story. The night was short if we didn't go to town. When we did go, we hated taking time to shed the farm dust and change clothes. Rick and I parked in the new Security State Bank parking lot, drank beer, smoked joints and listened to KOJM 6.10 radio, waiting for someone to show up and get the party started.

When the fall harvest was over, our drinking adventures slowed accordingly. The chill of winter shivered my bones as I sat at home, alone in the dark. Chic had moved from the north side to the apartment above the Main Street Barber Shop. My brother and Oscar Moran were inseparable drinking partners. They struggled for prolific resolution of developmental intimacy and isolation issues. They usually drank Animal Beer and rode the grub line, in that order. The first Christmas on my own, I sat in the second story window eating a three-year-old can of commodity string beans for dinner. I sat and smoked cigarettes and pegi', wondering how my mom was doing. How did things get so fucked up? "Is there free will, or is our fate sealed?" I asked myself. My locus of control focused on the externalization of the present condition. If only I had listened to Victor…I should have saved my money and forgotten about all the fun to be had.

I started thinking about my dad's way of life, his anti-Indian rhetoric expressed to me through his cowboy boots, belt, hat and shirts. The statements about how real men pulled themselves up by their boot straps…his loathing of the reservation, although he rarely stepped a foot on reservation land in my lifetime. He didn't hear my pleas because I was an Indian, a disappointment and a reminder of being native himself. Johnny Ball loved living in the white world and only came home a few times a year. After all, he was important running the white men's ranches. My parents discouraged participation in pow-wows or other native activities. Dad made it painfully obvious that being a Native meant you did not have boot straps and could never earn them. My problem was that he was half Indian, and so was my mom. I look native; I am native. Neither of my parents were "registered" with the Bureau of Indian Affairs due to Wakan Lokahe Win, First Holy Woman's kidnapping. I was never taught Indian values, so consequently I had no connection with or urge to join men like Russell Means in the American Indian Movement. I had my head up my ass. All the generations after the genocide, Indian children were beaten to remove those values, and generations later the values were no longer taught. We looked like Indians but we all tried to be white guys. I couldn't wait for Christmas day to be over…for the drinking to resume.

The 'honorary tribal member" was well established in my family history. Bartholomew Ball imbibed the alcohol spirit frequently after the Civil war. Alcohol was evil and foreign to First Holy Woman. It took a few generations for the demon to gain reverence. My father, his brothers and uncles succumbed to the seduction of the alcohol spirits. I was not above the inducement to alcohol and became immersed in the exercise of poor judgment at an early age. Fortunately, I eventually found my Irish spirit, Sitting Bull and Crazy Horse spirituality and moved on.

All this became my family's historical trauma – the kidnapping, fear, brutality, the addictions handed down to subsequent generations. Our family's emotional genocide began when an Irishman found his way west. After stealing Wakan Lokahe Win in the middle of the night, Bartholomew married her, taking away her true name and identity. The government policy and Indian agent insisted she have a white name when they got married. My great-grandfather gave his young wife his mother's and sister's first names, leaving the Lakota world behind. Even though First Holy Woman was full blood Lakota, the government told her otherwise. She officially became a white woman married to her white Irish husband and she gave birth to their *red shadows.* Perhaps people should have accepted her for more than a 'full blood squaw'.

The west was filled with people from around the globe, but Mary Jane Ball was undeniably Lakota, and that was difficult for a 'squaw man' to disguise with a pack of half-breed youngsters tagging behind. Throughout their time together, the relationship was plagued with fear of the U.S. Government and attempts to escape from its Auschwitz and Dachau impositions. Bartholomew and First Holy Woman's children were sent to schools among the white people; briefly attending Pratt's Model School in Carlisle Pennsylvania in spite of First Holy Woman's objections. For the year spent in Pennsylvania the children endured abuse in the Indian boarding schools. My great-grandparents' survival there and their travels with children across the nation became a testament to Bartholomew's "pull yourself up by the bootstraps" Irish stubbornness and First Holy Woman's Lakota philosophies and ideologies of the life cycle, from the blood moon birth to a life and death with honor.

Chapter 20

Where Are We Now?

The trauma my family and so many others experienced was all because of the white man's need to "own" the land and his inability to understand our ways. How was it that the U.S. Government determined who Indians were as a people? How did they legislate our future and issue false *Certificate of Indian Blood* registrations? It was obvious that Manifest Destiny would not be denied and that Indians were indeed a problem that needed to be dealt with. The intent of the Dawes Act of 1887 had been to civilize Indians, one by one if necessary. Indian land ownership was the focus of this type of legislation which assured, over time, that the government could claim ownership of tribal land due to thinning of the native blood. The government policy at that time was "Kill the Indian…Save the man". Generations later treatment of Indian people garnered the sympathies of liberal America, and the simplicity of genocidal extermination as a solution had since slipped away.

Prejudices eventually became more subtle. Indian children suffered the wrath of the white men and women who taught their children to berate and bully those filthy half breed 'injuns'. You could be any brand of degenerate reprobate, but nothing was lower than an Indian. We were considered the lowest, most despicable vermin to walk the Milk River Valley. It is still true in some places today.

As the modern solution to the "Indian Problem" morphed from genocide to assimilation, civilization was universally understood as life lived indoors, wearing civilized clothes, farming the ground, riding in Studebaker wagons, sending children to school, drinking whiskey, and owning land. Over time, it was disastrous for us to assume this white man's civilization. It cost us our lives, our culture, and our land.

So the story ends much like it began with fear, violence and brutality and in the end a genocide of the Native American Spirit. Qua Que watches, saddened by the white man's deeds and the Indians inability to stabilize. Loss is common to all Indian people, including the loss of our family histories and ancient oral tradition. My family's story is just one glimpse into the life of thousands of brown men who raise their families in the *red shadow* of this transgenerational historical trauma. Every Indian story is a sad story.

About The Author: by Margarett Campbell, Ed. D.

"I always knew Big John was different but I didn't know why nor did I think about it much. His thinking was on a different level than most high school kids, he had knowledge that I didn't understand. In many ways he was like an old man in a young man's body. The questions he asked our teachers were on a different level than us; they were complex and answers were scarce because our teachers didn't understand any of us, particularly someone with the level of intellect John was blessed. It wasn't until I was 60 years old and read his rich family history that I understood him and know why he was different, in a good way. He was from the wrong side of the tracks. Big John was not your run-of-the-mill Indian boy. He was different, his mind was sophisticated and knowledgeable of aspects of life that most teenagers never gave a minute of thought. Why did I wait until I read his book to understand him? His compassion and humility defined him as a very unique and wonderful person. At a very young age he figured out the social echelon in Harlem, the little border town to the Fort Belknap Indian Reservation. It was this understanding that shaped his adventurous life. Since that time the Civil Rights movement happened and many of the experiences Indian children had during the 50's and 60's no longer happen. Big John was there, he lived it, felt it and knew his place. He broke loose of the expected restraints and went on to live the life he led ... Rock band, Social Worker, Master's Degree, Rebel, Historian and author. I would anticipate perhaps "Red shadows of the Blood Moon" will become recommended reading for collegiate Native American Studies academic curriculum. Love you, Big John."

Margarett Campbell

About the Author by Bob Krech, MSW, LCSW

Havre Montana in the late 1980s was not a the most welcoming place to outsiders, or for that matter, locals from the neighboring Indian reservations of Rocky Boy and Fort Belknap. I recall distinctly sitting in the Hill County Courthouse Annex awaiting an initial interview to provide case work for Family and Youth Services. Fresh out of college, still idealistic and hopeful, I was nonetheless aware of the tensions between authorities and Indian Nations. As I sat waiting, a large and commanding man, clearly of Native American ethnicity crossed my path and we looked at one another. His gait was deliberate but his smile was kind, an opening to what would become an amazingly rich collaboration I enjoyed with John Wesley Contway over the next three decades.

Once hired, I was quickly acquainted with John in his capacity as Lead Investigator for the State of Montana on cases of child abuse and neglect. He was remarkably thorough and detail-oriented but with a determination to provide fair outcomes for the families he was appointed to investigate. His own upbringing on Fort Belknap gave him familiarity with and respect for cultural and family structures that nurture Indian children, institutions that don't necessarily conform to the State's requirements for child welfare. John's advocacy on behalf of families kept the best interest of children central while seeking to strengthen the cultural fiber that is essential for their identity and their futures.

John's path that led him to professional training in Social Welfare started as a young Indian child in the 1950s. John is a Sioux Native American born on the Ft Belknap Reservation and is the youngest of 10 children. He went to elementary and high school in Harlem Montana and while in his early teens cultivated his talent for music, forming a band with his friend Victor, which went by the name of The Freeman-Harper Band; a name arrived at during a period of enlightenment. He pursued a degree in Arts at the University of Montana, Missoula, graduating in 1985.

However, his awareness of the injustices suffered by Indian communities at the hands of the State drove him along another path, that included extensive coursework in social welfare and Native American studies. His experiences as a child on the reservation informed his professional development, recalling the anger and frustration of Indian families following interventions by the State justified according to the welfare of the children. Families were separated, children were placed in foster homes distant from the reservation, sometimes never to be seen again. John learned of the inequities between the State's management of Indian families and those of the dominant culture. In his determination to improve the lives of his community, John began a 30 year career in social work. He was first director of the Runaway and Homeless Youth Program on Fort Belknap. He soon moved to accept the position as Executive Director of ICWA with the Native American Service Center (now known as the Missoula Indian Center). Driven to have a greater impact on his community, he accepted a position as community social worker with the Montana Department of Family Services (DFS) in Havre, with responsibilities that later included supervision of social workers in two other counties and management of therapeutic treatment for Native American children who are severely emotionally disturbed.

Not content to limit his impact to the families assigned to him, John realized structural changes were need if Indian families were to benefit from State interventions regarding their welfare. His anger and determination drove him to advocate successfully to the State of Montana to transfer jurisdiction for all ICWA, CPS and foster care responsibilities from the state to the Indian nation at Fort Belknap (in 1997). John successfully pursued an appeal to the US Department of the Interior to ensure direct funding for ICWA child welfare activities to Fort Belknap, a model now adopted by other states.

John's determination to achieve structural change in welfare policy led him to pursue graduate work with Walla Walla College where he was awarded a Master's Degree in Social Work in 2002. After completing his degree, he accepted a position as lone Mental Health provider for the Aleutian populations on St. Paul and St. George in the Pribilof Islands in Alaska where he served for 7 years. During this time the Author was faced with many of the same problems he was familiar with on the reservation such as suicide, substance abuse, physical and sexual abuses, discrimination, and poverty, underscoring the structural inequities whose manifestations were felt by individuals.

John's experiences with Native Americans at the hands of the dominant culture, in both Alaska and Montana inform his narrative, "Red Shadows of the Blood Moon." It is a collection of 60 years of life coming to terms with his place in a sometimes-strange land. You will laugh, you will cry, THINK as you weave your way through a life lived.

Bob Krech

Printed in the United States
By Bookmasters